Praise for *U*

Miles Olson is a true radical; the problem—which is that w our own innate wildness and are busily trying to domesticate a planet that has a will of its own. The only real solution is to return to a wilder and simpler existence. Olson's pure, clear voice helps us get grounded and get started.

— Richard Heinberg, Senior Fellow, Post Carbon Institute, and author of *The End of Growth*

Unlearn, Rewild is an extraordinary and unconventional survival guide. Olson provides a hands-on manual to break free from enslavement to jobs, bills, and the trap of civilization to rediscover one's true nature.

— Thomas J. Elpel, author of *Participating in Nature*

Miles Olson has asked the all-important but often ignored question about sustainability: what kind of world do we wish to sustain? He then tears up some popular delusions about getting there.

— Samuel Thayer, author of *The Forager's Harvest*

Do the terms "human monoculture," "technology trap" or "ecocide" resonate with you? Are you going broke but want to live well? Does living outside the system appeal to you? Take this book, written by a professional dropout/escape artist, as you make your own escape. Along with philosophy (for attitude adjustment) it covers scavenging road kill, which grubs are good to eat and most everything else you need to know to go feral safely and in style.

— Dmitry Orlov, author of *Reinventing Collapse* and *The Five Stages of Collapse*, ClubOrlov.com

Unlearn,
Rewild

Unlearn, Rewild

Miles Olson

new society
PUBLISHERS

Cover design by Diane McIntosh. Images: © iStock

Printed in Canada. First printing July 2012.
Short-run printing 2019.

New Society Publishers acknowledges the support of the
Government of Canada through the Book Publishing Industry
Development Program (BPIDP) for our publishing activities.

Paperback ISBN: 978-0-86571-721-3
Ebook ISBN: 978-1-55092-517-3

Inquiries regarding requests to reprint all or part of *Unlearn, Rewild*
should be addressed to New Society Publishers at the address below.

To order directly from the publishers, please call toll-free
(North America) 1-800-567-6772, or order online at www.newsociety.com

Any other inquiries can be directed by mail to:

New Society Publishers
P.O. Box 189, Gabriola Island, BC V0R 1X0, Canada
(250) 247-9737

This book is intended to be educational and informative. It is not intended to serve
as a guide. The author and publisher disclaim all responsibility for any liability, loss or risk
that may be associated with the application of any of the contents of the book.

LIBRARY AND ARCHIVES CANADA CATALOGUING IN PUBLICATION

Olson, Miles
Unlearn, rewild / Miles Olson.

Includes index.
ISBN 978-0-86571-721-3

1. Wilderness survival. 2. Subsistence hunting.
3. Wild foods. 4. Sustainable living. 5. Self-reliance.
I. Title.

GV200.5.O47 2012   613.6'9   C2012-903703-6

New Society Publishers' mission is to publish books that contribute in fundamental
ways to building an ecologically sustainable and just society, and to do so with the
least possible impact on the environment, in a manner that models this vision. We are
committed to doing this not just through education, but through action. New Society
also works to reduce its carbon footprint, and purchases carbon offsets based on an
annual audit to ensure a carbon neutral footprint. For further information, or to browse
our full list of books and purchase securely, visit our website at: www.newsociety.com

Contents

Acknowledgments

This book would not exist had I not been the incredibly fortunate member of a community of rewilding humans over the past seven years. To all of the amazing people that make up this scattered clan of orphans, thank you.

My deepest gratitude to all of the friends and family that have supported me as a dropout and ne'er-do-well. In particular, Milota, an amazing comrade with whom I realized some of my wildest dreams. Lonnie and Levon, my brothers, thank you both for being there. My parents, for teaching me to live with integrity and think for myself, though not realizing where that might lead. A special thanks to Kevin Hodgson, for reminding me who I am and blowing the ember that became this book into flame. To Daniel, for "getting Miles into the woods" as you say, and being a friend through the ages. A thousand golden sun salutations to Jessi Junkin, whose care, love and comradery kept me warm and inspired while writing this. To the countless others that have shared love, pain, honesty, laughter and inspiration with me, thank you.

To the bats of Maurelle Island, the porcupines of Tagish, the countless blacktail deer, the Pentlatch River, the red alders, the cougars and many others who share ancient wisdom and make this world alive, thank you.

Introduction

This book is part philosophical treatise, part survival guide, part post-industrial living manual, part invitation to connect in a deep, meaningful way with the land. An invitation to heal ourselves and the Earth and bridge the gap between wildness and human existence. It is the result of many years spent living in the woods, at the edge of a small city with a group of friends in cabins that we built from scavenged materials on land we squatted. Years spent learning how to live intimately on the land, coming from a time and place where we've had to start from scratch, with no roots, no elders, no intact culture or teachers to guide us. Many hard lessons have been learned through trial and error.

This is a distillation of the most pertinent skills and ideas that have blossomed as a result, written largely by the warmth of fire and the glow of lamplight, in a homey squat that allowed us to bring some of our wildest dreams alive.

It takes for granted that humans want to live meaningful lives, that we want to live with integrity and that we don't want to kill the planet. That for the human animal to be sane, we *need* to have deep connections to the Earth. It is about action. More than just food for thought, these pages offer strategies, skills and ideas for changing our lives.

I have divided it into two parts, the first, "Ideas," and the second, "Endangered Skills."

The reason for this is that without a healthy context to practice them in, these skills are at best pointless, at worst destructive. Likewise, if philosophy doesn't translate into action, it is useless. You can't have one without the other.

This book presents a challenge. It asks us to look at hard truths. To look at how deep our collective problems really are. To not be distracted or dissuaded by industrial society's sad attempts to fake a transition to "green" energy and a seamless march towards a sustainable new world. To grapple with the problem of civilization at its roots, and our place within that problem. It also extends an invitation to rewild — to become part of the dance of this living land. To build independence and autonomy from the system, stepping into interconnectedness with non-humans and humans alike. To look at ourselves, our relationships and all of life through undomesticated eyes. To heal broken land, minds and hearts.

As I write this, the economies of all the great empires of the world are being bailed and beaten, wars are being fought over oil, arctic ice is rapidly in retreat, radioactive fallout is contaminating the rain, revolutions and riots are erupting worldwide as the wealth of nations shrinks and the divide between rich and poor rapidly grows to a boiling point. The future looks extremely uncertain from every angle.

To assume that the system is going to crumble, that any day now the forces threatening life on Earth will grind to a halt and stop leaving us free to live a more simple life, is not strategically wise. Neither is it wise to assume that the system is going to continue as it has been, that a way of life based on perpetual growth, massive inequality, ecological degradation, precarious technologies and ridiculous wastefulness can continue unchecked.

These pages offer skills for coping with changing times that could save lives, feed families and give us autonomy from increasingly oppressive regimes. Skills, also, for any time one chooses to connect with the wildness that is life. "Hardcore" sustainability skills, for a sustainable future that does not include industrial technology and production—a world most of us are afraid to imagine, but that is, eventually, inevitable.

This book is about reclaiming our future, our sanity, our ability to live in the land, our ability to live with integrity.

Scientists and authors have been saying for decades, "If we don't change things in the next few years, it'll be too late!" The time for those warnings has long passed. The reality is that in any relationship it is time to change things the moment they become unhealthy. If that moment has passed, the time is now—and has been for a while.

For Wild Aliveness.

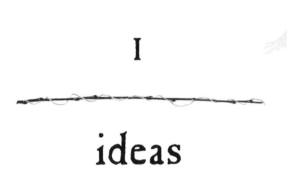

I

ideas

CHAPTER 1

Sustainability and Wildness

*The only war that matters
is the war against wildness.
All other wars are subsumed by it.*

Wildness

Everything on this Earth is inherently wild. If it lives and dies, it is part of the wildness that is life. Our word "will" is rooted in the word "wild"; the will of a creature, the will of the land— the driving force at its essence is its wildness. In a culture built on denying this truth, we tend to think of wildness as an exception, as something that exists in isolated pockets of wilderness here and there. Wildness is the rule, not the exception. Where it exists, it either lives unhindered in a wild state or is the victim of domestication. The keyboard I type these words on comes from different parts of this wild Earth, tortured and mangled together into the image of a keyboard. Everything has will—a desire for how it wants to exist and express itself. Everything is inherently wild.

Domestication

Domestication is what we are often surrounded by. It is also something that has happened to us, so it's not surprising that we don't notice it. "Domestication" is a pretty, polite word for a violent process. It might be better called "killing the wildness" since that's what it means. A domesticated creature is one that lives according to its human master's will, not its own. The more that creature (plant, land, river, etc.) can be made to forget its own will, its instinctual longings, the easier for its master to maintain control. If the cattle forget that they had ever known anything other than the feedlot, they won't feel confined.

How is domestication a violent process? A living thing's wildness is something potent: its strength lies in every cell of the body. Nothing was born to live in captivity, to be tamed, subdued and made submissive, and nothing accepts such a role without being forced. In order for a field of wheat to grow, every other living thing in that space must be eradicated. The field is tilled, loosening up the soil (that it can wash away), chemical fertilizer is applied, irrigation, pesticides, all to keep the field from remembering how it wants to live. Year after year, the field is ploughed, planted and sprayed, consuming enormous amounts of energy, because year after year it wants to go wild, to remember, to heal, and must be beaten into submission.

Once human societies start domesticating each other and their land bases, that is, violating and smothering their will, the process seems to become obsessive; it feeds itself. A look around should prove the point. It may be that humans began domesticating and developing agricultural societies with beautiful intentions, but once the process of taking wild space and turning it into human-designed "production" begins, things go out of control. Humans are capable of taking forests — home to countless species of plant, animal, bird, insect, mycelium — and after killing their wildness (removing the trees, turning the soil), converting it all into a production space for human food. The possibilities of expansion are limited only by how much suitable earth there is to exploit.

The final dream of civilization is that everything will be controlled, organized, categorized; all wildness and spontaneity will be eradicated. Fish will live in fish farms. Trees will grow in tree farms. Animals for our food will live in feedlots. Humans will live in cities completely isolated from any other creatures (except cute pets), isolated from anything that might remind them of true wild nature. "Inferior races" will wither in poverty until they vanish. The Earth will be remodeled in the name of production. Any spontaneous, uncontrolled expression of life will be crushed.

Of course, it isn't really the future I am describing.

Sustainability

How does this relate to sustainability? Is domestication unsustainable? I would say yes, but that isn't the issue I want to talk about here. There is a lot of buzz in mainstream society right now about who's "going green," about how industrial society is voluntarily making the transition to green energy and thus becoming sustainable.

Let's look at an example. The Brazilian rainforest is being cleared at an alarming rate to make way for vast plantations of soybeans. Hundreds of thousands of acres of genetically modified monoculture. What if those tractors were powered by biodiesel? What if they were powered by methane trapped from composting human feces, which was then used to fertilize the field? Imagine that picture as an example of sustainability—vegan food being farmed using green fuel and human compost.

But why would anyone want to sustain that?

The popular concept of sustainability paints a picture something like this: Humans are burning too much fossil fuel. There is nothing fundamentally wrong with how we live, or how we interact with this Earth, there are just some glitches in the system. Acidifying oceans, ozone holes and, most importantly, global warming. If we can only make a few simple changes—switch to green energy, organic farming, cloth bags instead of plastic, phase out fossil fuels—the Earth won't burn and industrial civilization will be able to continue indefinitely. I don't want to argue too much right here over whether it is *possible* for this culture to become sustainable. I think it is more important that we consider if it is even *desirable*! In the sustainability movement, there is no discussion on *what it is we want to make sustainable*, or even what has been sustainable in the past. A culture of hunter-gatherers lived sustainably for thousands of years in the Brazilian rainforest I mentioned above, that is now eradicated and subdued into producing soybeans for the eco-conscious North American. Can a domesticated, modern human have any concept of what is sustainable, being so removed from any real point of reference? Remember, one of the most important parts of being domesticated is forgetting your wild nature, or having those memories erased of who you are and what you need at the most primal level.

The only proven models we have for existing sustainably as humans (the only way humans have ever actually existed sustainably) are hunter-gatherer societies. These cultures did, and do, cultivate their land bases in many subtle ways, the important difference from agricultural society being that they directly depend on the health of their wild land base while agricultural society depends on fighting and destroying it. One way preserves the land, the other rapidly destroys it. Hunter-gatherers are tied to a limited resource base; a culture that kills too many bison will soon starve. This gives them an incentive to not get too big or too greedy. If an agricultural society gets too big or greedy, it just clears more land to plant more grain and so on and on, until…it becomes sustainable?

What do We Want to Make Sustainable?

This is a very important question. Do we want to continue to abuse all life on this planet, making it conform to our twisted visions of what is needed? Do we want to have a sustainable human-engineered Earth, completely ordered and controlled to maximize efficiency? A sustainable world where everyone and everything is tagged, drugged, kept submissive, orderly, tame? Or do we want to give up on the project of controlling all life on Earth? Becoming sustainable does not mean allowing the wildness of living things to flourish, letting blackberries and dandelions grow through the concrete, turning the pavement into soil (and food!).

It doesn't mean healing our relationship with the land, ourselves or each other. In fact, the popular concept of sustainability, if enacted, would simply mean making the war against wildness perpetual. Domestication is the root of the giant chasm between humans and the non-human world, it is the engine that propels us towards killing the planet. Yet, somehow, it has completely snuck under the radar of the ongoing discussion on "going green," probably because it is a much more ancient and deeply rooted problem than burning fossil fuels. It makes the solution much more complex.

The ancient civilization of what is now called Iraq successfully deforested rainforests of giant cedars, planted them with wheat and turned them into desert in just a few centuries using primitive stone, bone and wood tools, as well as farming organically. Phasing out fossil fuels isn't enough. Going back to a pre-industrial level of technology isn't enough. There is a sickness at the heart of this culture, something very powerful and destructive that we need to see. We need to enter into a conversation with the land we take from in order to live and allow ourselves to hear its screams. We need to have relationships that aren't manipulative and abusive, with one another and the Earth. "Sustainability" is not primary, it might even be a destructive goal. That wild aliveness flourish is what matters.

The only war that matters
is the war against wildness.
All other wars are subsumed by it.

CHAPTER 2

What is Rewilding?

Picture a vacant parking lot in a part of town that has been abandoned. After a year or so every crack big enough has given way to dandelions and the young beginnings of blackberry vines. The action of their roots, the wind and rain, water pooling in between tiny nooks, freezing and thawing, slowly crack and crumble the pavement. Fissures split wider making space for more plants, more roots, more cracks. The pavement itself is soon no longer visible under the thick foliage of briars and alder saplings during the summer months. Birds begin nesting in the shrubs, rabbits under the barbed wire protection of the blackberry vines.

After a few decades, the land will have shrugged off much of its cement blanket. Trees will be sending their taproots deep into the soil, and though it will still carry the fresh wounds of having been brutally forced into the shape of a parking lot, it will be well on its way to recovering and returning to a healthy, wild state.

Now picture a human…

Rewilding is not a term commonly applied to humans. The process of a species or ecosystem returning to a natural, untamed state isn't exactly the direction much of humanity is currently headed in. Rewilding stands opposite to domestication. Where domestication means domination, control, oppression and eradication of what does not submit, rewilding means breaking free from these elements and working against them, enabling others (human and non-human) to escape oppression and live with integrity. At its essence, the wildness, the life force in everything domesticated is fighting to express itself, to find a crack, sprout and grow; to find a hole in the fence and make a break. This includes humans.

Rewild, v : to return to a more natural or wild state; the process of undoing domestication.
Synonyms: undomesticate, **uncivilize.**

Of course many humans would disagree that we are domesticated. This is not surprising; a true, fully domesticated creature wouldn't have any idea that things are not normal and natural, that something is off.

I once did a work trade with a bison farmer who lives near me, cutting Scotch broom from his pastures in exchange for meat, fat and bones. Besides being in awe of and somewhat terrified by all the massive, intimidating, beautiful horned beasts casually tromping around me, the most amazing thing I found about the whole experience was the fence that contained these bison. All that kept them contained in the farmer's fields was lightweight wire deer fencing. The farmer told me proudly one day: "Oh ya, those bison could charge right through that fence, no problem. It's just psychology, you know, ya get 'em used to something and they don't even think about it!"

The bison could have left, they could have gone on the endless migration their bodies and spirits are meant for instead of being confined to that puny, overgrazed pasture, but their conditioning kept them from ever trying.

To rewild necessarily means understanding and unlearning our conditioning, the cultural programming that determines how we see and interact with the world. If you are reading this, you are literate, meaning you have certainly been enculturated, indoctrinated and assimilated, to some extent, by the dominant culture. You have been trained to see the world through its filters. To believe that humans are not animals; that animals do not think or feel or speak. That humans have "intelligence" and it is unique to us. That the "natural" world is separate from the "human" world and exists as an inexhaustible pool of "resources" for human consumption. That you work, you pay rent, you buy food. You don't ask why, that is just how it is. That jobs are good, jobs mean money, and money is good. That we *need* money to live. Pieces of paper or numbers in a computer system—we *need* it more than life itself. That we want the "economy" always to grow. That if the economy (a measure of our physical toll on the natural world) doesn't grow, we are doomed. That there are many things you need (money, car, job, status) and without them you won't have any friends. No one will have sex with you. That our bodies and minds are separate. That our bodies are disgusting, our desires also. That women are inferior to men. That it's you with the problem, it's you that is insane, not this world—take a pill.

We are trained from a very early age to respond to bells and whistles, to accept this culture's version of reality as truth without question. The process of rewilding is the process of unlearning all of this, coming to know an unmediated reality based on real life interaction, empathy and experience.

The Human Creature

Humans are extremely adaptable. Our minds quickly adjust to new environments and living situations. We are fundamentally still Stone Age creatures living in an industrial world, our biology having changed very little in the last 10,000 years. If you took a twenty-first century newborn and swapped him or her with a hunter-gatherer newborn, both would learn how to live based on the cultures that surround them and thrive equally.

Our adaptability has allowed us to inhabit the Earth, it has allowed cultures to thrive in desert, high Arctic, temperate rainforest and tropical jungle. It has allowed us to rapidly incorporate new technologies and gracefully adapt to isolating modern living conditions though antidepressants, the Internet, alcohol, pornography and other drugs help ease the void such an industrial life inevitably leaves. Our constant adaptation often leaves us wondering where we come from and who we are; what is the natural way for a human to live? Does that even exist? Do we have inherent needs? Does anything?

I used to hate the saying, "Humans are social creatures." I was a loner growing up, and as a teenager fascinated by Buddhism—the ideal of living a solitary, monastic life in pursuit of enlightenment. I didn't see why people insisted that humans are social creatures; society is awful.

It wasn't until I was 20 or so that I put it together, by looking at the only examples of healthy humans I was aware of—indigenous people. Humans have always lived in groups. Bison have always lived in herds, seagulls live in flocks, crows live in murders, wolves roam in packs, and for human creatures to be healthy, they need to live in a group, a community, a tribe. They (we) always have. Solitary confinement is used as a form of torture, often driving the victim pathologically insane; meaningful social interaction and community are a biological *need*.

Industrial society *is* awful, I just got it and society in general confused, having that as the only visible society to reference. Humans are not industrial creatures, there is no such thing as an industrial creature (with the possible exception of

Monsanto's genetically modified creations), but we absolutely are social creatures. It is how we have evolved; humans have always lived in tribes or extended family units. The fact that it took me 20 years of human life to realize this speaks volumes on how far we have come from something healthy and intact.

Humans, along with all other creatures, have also always lived in intimate physical contact with their life source, the land. This is another inherent need; as much as we need to have healthy, deep interactions with humans, we need to have healthy, deep interactions with non-humans. We have evolved to live meaningful lives, in communities with young and old, harvesting food to eat and share, killing plants and animals to live, watching elders die, building our own homes, keeping them warm, learning the stories of the mountains and rivers and ancestors.

It goes without saying that industrial life lacks all of these; it leaves our lives isolated, disconnected, shallow and meaningless. Humans have not evolved to build a perpetually growing economy (nothing alive on this planet can support that delusion), live in cities, organize ourselves through large centralized power structures, spend our days idle behind desks and screens, repeat mundane tasks, or even farm. We suck at all of these things, actually, and are killing the planet and have collectively gone insane as a result.

Civilization

> *"The house is on fire, what are you going to do?"*
> *"Add some fuel to the flames and watch to see if something beautiful grows from the ashes."*

Civilizations are those cultures based on the domestication of plants, animals and humans. Farming, imperialism, social stratification and the creation of towns and cities are their trademarks. The human sacrifices of the Aztecs, the inquisition bonfires of old Europe and the Nazi holocaust were all the work of civilized peoples; genocide is part of their mode of operations. The perpetrators of genocide have even historically called it the process of "civilizing" their victims. Though scholars and the religious often pat civilization on the back for its moral superiority, no other culture has enacted atrocities on anywhere near the scale of this one. Rape, for instance, was completely unknown to most all Native American cultures. There is an old tale of when Nuu-chah-nulth tribespeople found the dead, naked, violated bodies of two young girls that had been raped by Spanish conquistadores in the woods near their village; they were dumbfounded. Nothing like this had ever happened, it was not part of their reality. European colonists were astonished by this, rape being such a fundamental part of civilized society.

Unlike sustainable cultures, civilizations have a short life, exhausting their land base and collapsing or moving on. Ever notice how if the economy isn't growing, it's collapsing? If GDP doesn't perpetually grow, the system constantly expand, there is a "depression"? Civilization is based on expansion. It is either growing or it is dying; there is no steady, stable state. Driven by a population boom that began with the agricultural revolution and has yet to level off, its perpetual expansion means perpetual conquest. In order for it to continuously grow, others must be displaced; indigenous cultures, forests, prairies, wetlands, rivers, all occupy potential sites for resource extraction, cities and farms. They must be eliminated, controlled or assimilated in order for progress to continue.

It should go without saying that a system based on perpetual expansion cannot exist for long on a finite planet. Humans have only been building civilizations for 6000 years; for 95.5 percent of our existence on Earth we have lived in place-based, sustainable societies. Only recently has the dominant culture nearly completely eradicated and assimilated the majority of these unique ways of being. What most of us fail to realize is that the problem of perpetual growth is not a contemporary one. It is not the creation of capitalism or the corporation, though they have put it into overdrive. The problem of perpetual growth is as old as civilization. It is *the* problem of civilization, a way of life that is functionally unsustainable; it can vary in how quickly it destroys, but it always has been and always will be destructive.

Essentially a failed 6,000-year experiment, civilization has nearly completely eradicated all cultures but itself, and now is working at eliminating all life on the planet.

Rewilding is not about saving civilization. From the perspective of a wild, living creature, there is absolutely nothing worth redeeming about civilization. Based on the suppression of human and non-human wildness, including deforestation and desertification, from a biological standpoint, civilization is a cancer on the earth. It is the perfect example of humans creating technologies but not having the ability or maturity to control them.

When faced with the prospect of collapse, many in the sustainability movement fear that civilization will crumble and we will lose all of the advancements it has bestowed upon us (scientific knowledge, art, vaccinations, etc.). "We need to build lifeboats for civilization, do whatever it takes to save it!" Implicit in this urge is that "uncivilized" people's lives are worse than ours.

Indigenous cultures enjoy better health, more leisure time, more egalitarian social structures than civilized people. Hunter-gatherers in the Kalahari desert, for example, who inhabit an extremely marginal landscape, put in an average three-hour work day, are free from tooth decay and other degenerative conditions, are healthier and have more free time than industrial people. When Europeans began their invasion of the Americas in the 16th century, the "Old World" was an overpopulated wasteland of human depravity, on the brink of collapse with famine, warfare and epidemics being the norm. The indigenous cultures of the "New World," in contrast, were as a rule physically healthier, had more breathing room and a much higher standard of living. The idea that civilized life is easier, healthier and innately better than any other way of living is something we must unlearn.

Traditionally, every landscape, every climate, every bioregion has given birth to a diverse culture that fit uniquely into it; there has never been one way of living that made sense for every place. Rewilding is a movement towards reconnecting with place, growing roots and dedicating ourselves to a bioregion, slowly learning how to live in that place in a way that fits into its rhythms.

A Clean Mind

If you remove a dam from a river, it will spill, flood and flow freely. If you let cattle out of their cages, they will roam, graze, live and die freely. If you let a human out of its captivity, it will...? Look for a job? Become a dumpster-diving vagabond? Go wild and free in the wilderness? Humans are quite unpredictable, and how they respond to freedom is complicated.

We are extremely cerebral. Where some creatures are physically adapted to their environment with fur, claws, webbed feet, fins or wings, humans have sadly ill-adapted bodies, for which we compensate with overactive brains. No doubt our domestication is partly physical: our feeble bodies and the masters' guards (police, military) disable us and ensure we stay well-behaved; but, being such cerebral creatures, it is also enormously psychological. Many of the shackles that keep the domesticated human in place are not physical at all, but invisible, culturally created illusions. Our job is to unlearn these illusions, to clean our minds.

Everyone has different wounds to heal from, everyone has different ways of healing.

Being alone in nature has been, in my experience, one of the most powerful tools for unlearning conditioning. Most traditional cultures use the experience of going alone into wild nature as a tool for cleaning the mind, washing a culturally constructed reality from one's consciousness and allowing one to have real, unmediated interaction with the more-than-human world. It is part of becoming a whole person, seeing life with clarity, a rite of passage.

When I was 17, having just left high school and many years of heartbreaking boredom and bullshit, I spent a summer living alone in the woods on a small, isolated island. With no electricity, no running water, no people around, and lots of free time, I had one of the most intense experiences of unlearning in my life. At first I was afraid and my mind was paranoid. I heard cougars in the woods — nature was out to get me. I had to stay on high alert or die in its cruel grip. Then I became lonely and sad. I thought I was missing life by being alone in the woods. Eventually I started simply existing, picking berries, hauling water to my little veggie patch. Eventually I watched my mind become quiet. I watched plants grow. I watched the stars at night and slept beneath them. I dried berries under the sun. Things existed that I had never known were there.

I remember, after not having talked to anyone for a week or two, trying to remember what my name was. I walked around the cabin where I was staying for an hour searching for something that had my name on it so I could be reminded. My mind had become quiet and my relationship with life ecstatic. I unlearned so much that summer.

People in healthy cultures undertake this type of practice from time to time. Solitude is not a glorified way of life, but a method of cleansing so that you can come back to your community stronger, saner and wiser, to share your gifts more fully.

Even taking an hour every now and then and being alone with wild nature, letting your mind slow down and step outside its illusions, to listen and watch, can be profoundly healing.

There are as many ways to clean our minds, to unlearn, as there are people. For anyone wanting to be sane and of service to their community, it is vital they find what will work for them.

Rewilding our minds, hearts and bodies is a lifelong journey. To create healthy cultures is probably going to take many lifetimes. That doesn't mean we have to wait; we'll actually need to be working at it the whole time.

To go back to the example of the abandoned parking lot, the pavement, cracks, dandelions and blackberry vines; the pavement is this culture, the cracks are there and growing, we are the dandelion seeds blowing in the wind. Find a good crack to land in and start crumbling the pavement with your roots.

CHAPTER 3

Subsistence

They've been hunting here for ten thousand years...

MAYBE LONGER. The river has slowly changed its shape over that time; ancestors from long ago wouldn't recognize it as it flows now. It has meandered far, eroding and building, snaking across the land. They have learned the patterns of the deer, acorn and salmon; in the fall deer are fattest, acorns are ripe and salmon spawn, so they come here to camp every fall and at other times of the year, too.

From the acorns they make meal and bread; the salmon is smoked or eaten fresh; the deer's flesh they dry and make the skin into clothing, bowstrings and snares. Having long ago learned to eat and use what this land offers, it is abundant to them.

Every so many years the acorns aren't abundant, the deer in the following year may be scarce. The people are a reflection of the land, they are acorn, deer, huckleberry and salmon. If there are less acorn or deer, they will eat more salmon. If everything is scarce, they will have fewer children, eat more plants, some they might not eat normally. They will scrape through, though it may be hard.

Most of the plants and animals don't notice the people. The people don't bother them, don't have much to do with the many different grasses and lichens and tree frogs. Even many deer barely see them, avoiding the strong-smelling camps and villages.

The river often floods here late in the fall, when the big storms come. By then the people have moved to high ground, knowing the rhythms and moving with them.

Like all other living things, they are at the mercy of the land, there is no separation.

They have lived this way for a long time.

The longer they live here, the more stories there are, the more lessons passed down, the more steeped they become in the wisdom of this land and the knowledge of gracefully living within it.

They make the land yield…

In good years it is generous and bountiful, they ask for it to say "grain" and it obeys. But most years it wants to do as it pleases, it withholds and will not follow commands. Almost always now, if you let it, it withholds. Like a troublesome child that will not do as she is told, will not shut up and behave, when the land acts up like this it must be punished and brought into line.

They used to use tools of stone and bone, then metal tools, ploughs, irrigation; now they have drugs, chemicals synthesized in laboratories that will make it act as it should. They have discovered the secrets of the seed, breeding it to be obedient, breeding even their chemicals into it. They will make the land yield. It may be half dead and drugged, but it will nevertheless produce what they want.

Everything living here feels the people's presence. The voles are killed by the spraying. The gophers are killed by the combine harvester. The trees are gone. Glyphosate makes the grass drunk and confused. Is it dying? It's turning brown—but it's spring, not fall?

They divert the river to keep the land moist at all times. They build up levees around the river and dams to control its flow. Eventually they encase it in walls of cement and rebar. The river is held in place, it no longer meanders or floods; it is under control and put to use.

At harvest time the fields are stripped. They made this harvest—the land was a vessel for their creation.

The land is a servant, an ignorant waste without them. They make it yield.

They grow in number.

When the land is so disobedient that none of their efforts give results and the harvest is poor, the rich will stay fat—they have stored food from previous years and will keep the meager harvest. The poor will starve. Like the fields, they are simply servants.

One day the land will be depleted beyond exhaustion, its flesh barren and cracked. The people will then be done with it and move on.

Food and Culture

Eating food is the most intimate way a human can interact with the land.

It is how soil mixes with flesh, how we are inextricably linked. It only follows, then, that human cultures are shaped enormously by what they eat and how they get it. This defines how we interact with the land, each other and other cultures.

How a culture treats its land base, its relationship to non-humans, is reflected like a mirror in how it treats humans. Those that abuse the land abuse one other, those that dominate and subdue the land do so to their own. There is no separation.

It is common knowledge to anthropologists that societies defined as "hunter-gatherer" do not destroy their land bases, are free from hierarchical class structures (the powerful rich and the powerless poor), slavery, structured religion and many diseases of civilization. The more agricultural a society becomes, the greater the class divide and other oppressive elements such as institutionalized religion, strict gender roles, slavery, genital mutilation, imperialism, art and so on. Urbanization, deforestation and desertification are also synonymous with agriculture. One of the best illustrations of this is Marshall Sahlins' classic, *Stone Age Economics*.

I remember this point being hammered home years ago while I flipped through a book titled *Peoples and Cultures of Uganda*. The book provided details on subsistence patterns and social structures for dozens of cultures in present-day Uganda. Most of the people were agriculturalists, some were pastoralists (herders), some a mix of hunting and small farming, and a very few were hunter-gatherers living in the remaining forests. There was a shocking correlation between the level of cultivation and agriculture that these cultures practiced and oppressive behavior.

The forest-dwelling pygmies had no religion, art or warfare. They were egalitarian and had an incredibly light footprint on the land, building simple shelters during the rainy season that were barely perceptible to the outsider. Pastoral societies and those that relied on farming and some wild food had more complex religions—a tradition of fearing and killing "witches" was part of this—a loose class structure (by which I mean there was a division in wealth and power between elites and the commoners), art, an erosive relationship with soil and some small-scale warfare. The full-on agricultural societies had everything the last group had, but intensified. They were imperialistic and ecologically destructive, female genital mutilation was (and is?) the norm, institutionalized religion was enforced, and they had (and continue to have) serious issues with overpopulation, poverty and disease.

This is the general pattern, and I'm going to risk being redundant by repeating what I've already said: cultures that live by hunting, gathering and carefully tending or gardening their land bases have traditionally been sustainable. Those that practice farming have never been, anywhere, ever. Agriculture is the driving force behind human overpopulation and ecological degradation—nuclear disasters, global warming and the like are only issues because a society propped up by industrial agriculture is creating them. No other method of subsistence has produced anything remotely as destructive.

Agriculture Defined

Often it is stated that "agriculture *is* culture" or "there is no culture without agriculture." Farming is simply how humans get food; like bees and their flowers, it's part of the natural order. This we need to unlearn.

Agriculture: the cultivation (**culture**) of a field (Latin **ager** becomes **agri**).

Agriculture literally means "cultivating a field." This entails clearing land to make a field (no land is simply vacant and waiting for humans to take charge) and eradicating undesired species to plant the desired annual crops. It also means tilling the soil. It is something that humans have been practicing for about five percent of their existence here on Earth, yet in that five percent blip it has overtaken almost every other method of subsistence. In that five percent blip nearly all of the Earth's ancient forests have been felled and a mass extinction has been enacted. It hasn't overtaken other ways of living because it's better, it has done so because cultures that farm are inherently expansive and imperialistic. Agriculture is a contagious disease.

Some believe that agriculture and Western civilization are the result of addictive, opiate-like compounds in cereal grains, that farmers are the ultimate junkies, possessed by wheat, clearing more and more land to plant monocultures and themselves becoming and enacting a monoculture. Farming is, after all, calorie for calorie far more energy intensive than hunting and gathering—meaning it never actually made logical sense.

Instead of simply harvesting and processing foods, one must plow, plant, tend, irrigate, protect, harvest and process foods. It is not economically or ecologically an improvement on hunting and gathering, in fact it is a degeneration.

Pre-contact Iroquoian culture was based on farming corn, squash and beans. When researchers analyzed Iroquoian coprolites (stool samples) from this period, they found that the typical diet consisted of less than ten percent wild food. Even though wild food sources like deer, fish and acorns were definitely available, people were eating nearly exclusively the foods they produced via farming. There are even accounts of Iroquoian hunters targeting pregnant deer to reduce their population in efforts to control damage to corn fields.

Why the preference for agricultural food? Judging by the patterns of other agrarian cultures (including the one we are surrounded by), farming creates a tunnel-visioned perception of what "food" is: it blinds those practicing it to foods that are not farmed. Many wild foods are actually destructive to farm crops (deer, "weeds"), making them an enemy, even though they are just as much food as the plants being chosen as such. Food, of course, is a cultural construct, meaning that our culture teaches us that some things are food and some aren't. Grasshoppers are more nutritious, sustainable and actually taste better than soybeans, but our culture teaches that only one of them is food—and it happens to be the one that causes breast cancer and infertility, as documented by, among others, researchers at Michigan State University ("Estrogenic effects of genistein on the growth of estrogen receptor-positive human breast cancer (MCF-7) cells in vitro and in vivo," C.Y. Hsieh et. al.).

There is, of course variation in the pattern of slavery, ecocide and centralized power that coincides with agriculture.

Traditional cultures along the Northwest coast were by no means agricultural, but had such an abundant, easily harvested source of food, with the various species of salmon that returned to their rivers every year, among other marine and terrestrial foods, that they developed many characteristics usually attributed to full-blown civilizations. Slavery, a ruling elite, ritual head-binding among some groups and a culture of warfare are a few of the characteristics they possessed that are usually reserved for more "advanced" cultures. Northwest cultures, however, have a couple of major features that distinguish them from civilizations.

For one thing, they never destroyed their land bases. This might be related to the fact that their staple food, salmon, was wild, not cultivated. This means that the abundance of their food source was directly tied to the health of a rich, complex ecosystem, not clearing land to plant fields.

Secondly, they couldn't expand. Again this is related to their food source being tied to the rivers and shores. You can't conquer your weaker neighbors living inland (with no abundance of salmon to make them as strong and numerous as you), cut down the forests there and plant a river of spawning salmon in the clearing. Unlike the great expansive, imperialistic civilizations built on field crops (wheat, corn, rice, etc.), their central food source was immovable, and so were they. The fact that salmon is a wild food that requires healthy rivers and forests kept these cultures in check.

A culture that depends on the health of a wild land base will nurture it. A culture that depends on damaging that wild land base will undermine it.

At the end of the day we all depend on the health of our land base.

What about other, invisible forces that made sustainable cultures stay in balance? Spiritual practices, cultural taboos and the hugely significant fact that non-humans were respected, held sacred, communicated with and considered powerful, are attributes that are as, if not more, significant than the fact that some cultures physically couldn't expand. There is much to be learned here, considering we have the tools and knowledge to live so destructively.

For a way of subsistence that is sane to evolve, we are going to have to create cultures that reinforce healthy boundaries, that keep themselves in check.

I am certainly not suggesting that we can create a peaceful world simply by changing how we eat. The mechanisms of destruction in place are far too entrenched for that to happen. If we are going to move toward a sustainable future, however — and we have to — a major part of that is going to be redefining how we interact with the land, what we eat and how we get it.

Until we realize that our survival depends on the health of a wild land base, until we can again become an intimate part of that wild land base, we will continue killing the planet.

CHAPTER 4

Technology, Ethics and Freedom

Every technology begins as a key and ends as a cage.
« ran prieur »

A COUPLE OF YEARS AGO my friend was gifted a book
titled *Caribou Hunter.* It is the memoir of one of the last
great traditional Innu hunters, Mathieu Mestokosho, who
lived nomadically on the tundra of what is now called northern Quebec. I picked it up off the shelf and fell in love. Tales
of epic expeditions, herds of countless caribou, an intimate
knowledge of place and love for the caribou that sustained the
people kept me rapt. The most stunning story was of a hunting
party lost on the tundra without bedding, and as night closed
in they killed a number of caribou, skinned them and used
the fresh hides as warm blankets under the cold arctic night.
The stories took place during the early 20th century, long after
Mathieu's people had made contact with European civilization—they hunted exclusively with guns. This alone kept my
friend from reading the book as she had no respect for anyone
that used guns to hunt. I had no issue with the fact that guns
were their tool of choice, but it leads to an important question: what technologies are ethical, what technologies give too
unfair an advantage, which ones are inherently destructive and
does it really matter?

Technology and Disconnection

My good friend is not alone in her distaste for guns, of course. Many intelligent, caring people feel that using guns as a hunting (or combat) tool gives the user a ridiculous level of power. In the context of hunting, specifically, this power eliminates many natural checks and balances that might level the playing field between predator and prey. One needn't enter into the hunt so deeply if they have the power of a high-caliber rifle resting on its steel stand, outfitted with a scope that enables the shooter to reliably place their bullet from hundreds of yards away. Where once a hunter had to cover their scent (perhaps abstaining from certain odorous foods, sexual intimacy and other heavily scented activities for days before the hunt), move in silence and otherwise appease the prey's demands before being allowed to get within killing range, one can now drive to a good lookout, sit back for an hour and make the kill easy enough.

Every succeeding level of technology creates a further disconnect, with a simultaneous increase in power, control and efficiency—a troublesome combination. You can dig a hole much faster with a shovel than your hands, but you no longer feel the soil. You can cut a tree down much faster with a saw than stone tools, with a chainsaw than a hand saw, and with a feller-buncher than a chainsaw. In every stage the person doing the cutting becomes more removed from the process, more alienated from the individual tree that is being cut. You kill faster, feel less.

This is one of the traps of technology: what it gives in the form of power and efficiency, it takes away in the form of connection and understanding. More power plus less understanding equals a world of super-powered, infantile rednecks.

The real reason I didn't share my friend's condemnation of old Cree hunters using rifles instead of bows, is that the ones truly being victimized by this technology were not the caribou. The caribou were still free, the people had entered a trap.

A Deeper Critique

Of course, after being introduced, guns made bows obsolete because of their greater range and ease of maintenance, bullets being easier to buy and use than arrows were to make. Most indigenous people quickly forgot how to make bows and arrows from local material and, though still hunters, became fundamentally reliant on firearms and trade with Europeans for their survival. What began as a key rapidly turned into a cage. This is a universal effect of industrial, non-place-based technology: it destroys autonomy. We become slaves to those who control its source.

Automobiles allow humans to travel immense distances with no effort, in little time. Sounds pretty good, but on the down side, humans in car culture struggle with obesity, debt, depression, rage, auto-related fatalities and that nasty lingering fact that burning fossil fuels is killing the planet.

The Internet allows us to connect to each other in ways unimaginable in the past. On the other hand, it gives people a toxic imitation of real-life connection. It allows us to access massive amounts of information any time, any place. It seemingly destroys our brains' ability to retain that information, since it is being found outside of any real context. It poisons the sexuality of men, with its universally available and consumed misogynist pornography.

Every new technology promises to make life easier but in reality only creates a new dependency, a new level of complexity, a new poison. It becomes a crutch as we forget what we used to need to know: that eradication of practical knowledge is weakening and dangerous.

The only level of technology that is truly sustainable is place-based technology, or as it is commonly referred to, Stone Age technology. Any intensive mining is by definition unsustainable, because one is dealing with non-renewable resources. Therefore all steel, plastic, photovoltaics and otherwise modern tools are not sustainable. If you can't harvest it from the land without industrial tools, and if it doesn't regrow or replenish itself at a rate that keeps pace with the rate at which you harvest it, it can't be sustainable.

Would it be realistic to completely abandon all such tools?

No.

Would it be strategically wise?

Absolutely not. We are all coming from a place of being seriously caged in by technology. Moving towards a healthy level of technology—truly appropriate technology—is going to be a slow process.

Truly sustainable technologies are renewable and place based, meaning the necessary components can be harvested from one's bioregion, giving those with practical knowledge a deep level of autonomy or freedom.

Some manufactured tools have no sustainable equivalent (spaceships, cars, iPhones), some do (wheelbarrows, clothing, brooms, musical instruments, boxes). Even if industrial society were to cease functioning tomorrow, there would still be plenty of plastic buckets for 20–30 years (until they photodegrade, become brittle and fall apart) and steel tools for some time to come. The most strategically wise route would be to learn how to use and care for these tools properly, and then learn how to live without them. This might look like learning how to make oak barrels traditionally, while still keeping and using plastic or metal barrels. Learning how to make buckskin clothing but still rocking your favourite FUBU jersey. Learning how to use, sharpen and care for a cross-cut saw, and really scratching your head wondering what life would be like cutting firewood without steel tools.

While depending on industrial technology may be suicide, at this point completely giving it up one hundred percent might also be. As the saying goes: "Ideally we would use all of the master's tools to dismantle the master's house." After all, I wrote these words on a keyboard, you're reading them in the pages of a book, and this is all part of a movement away from industrial technology.

Is Technology Neutral?

It is often said that technology is neutral, it is neither inherently good or bad, healthy or destructive. It is inanimate and carries no energy of its own; it is only as good or bad as its user. "Guns don't kill people, people kill people." This may be true to a point, but I would be more inclined to say that technology is actually *never* neutral. Yes, people kill people, but people with guns kill a lot more people. Technologies evolve much faster than humans mature; for technology to be neutral, people would have to be immune to the seductive effect of power. I think it goes without saying that as a species, humans are not immune to the enticing lure of power that technology represents. In this sense, technologies have a power and momentum of their own; without a culture that keeps them in check, they are free to grow and grow, creating dependency and destruction, ultimately becoming a self-reinforcing trap.

Hypocrisy

The question of hypocrisy will always come up when we talk about these things. How can I criticize high technology and write a book on a laptop? Does this disqualify me as a hypocrite?

Is it hypocritical for the inmate of a prison to criticize the prison system? After all, they depend on the prison for their food and shelter.

The answer is an obvious no. The inmate only relies on the prison for food and shelter because they are trapped there. Similarly, we are trapped, navigating a world that has been broken, living amid a human monoculture that is highly technological and unsustainable. For most of us, completely eschewing the use of all this culture's unsustainable tools is actually not possible. Moving towards a simpler future, taking steps towards a truly healthy world is, but it's not going to happen overnight. Like a prison inmate, our escape is going to take careful planning and strategy. Again, we are going to have to use some of the master's tools to get free.

Puritanism is an awful strategy.

CHAPTER 5

How to Walk Away
from Civilization

O FTEN THOSE AMONG US disenchanted with industrial society, tired of the alienation, meaninglessness, destructiveness and boredom that characterize modern life, just want to walk away from it. There are some who think that a solution to the problem of civilization is for people to drop out, build something that works better, then wait for those still in the system to see the folly of their ways and change. I wouldn't go so far as to count myself among them.

Having spent many years as a dropout, a squatter living with others on the fringe of this culture by scavenging, gathering, hunting and gardening, I have developed a unique perspective on the possibilities, as well as the realities and obstacles to realizing this fantasy.

You Must — You Can't

There is no doubt that most humans on this planet, particularly in the Western world, need to live very differently than they currently do. A common misconception, though, is that there is a legitimate option that would let us enact this.

The dominant culture presents an illusion of choice: that we choose to work, we choose to pay rent, pay for food, pay for a car that we need in order to keep the job that we need in order to pay for shelter and food (our most basic necessities) that are otherwise under lock and key.

What happens if we opt out? What happens if we say "No, thanks. I'm not interested in that life, I'll just go over here and feed and house myself independently from you?"

This culture says: "Actually, no; you're either with us or you're against us."

As soon as you begin to act outside the system, you are breaking its rules. Being somewhere you do not own or have permission to be is "trespassing," eating food without paying for it is "stealing," hunting without the proper license and above the state-sanctioned amount is "poaching," simply sleeping somewhere is "vagrancy" or "squatting." Planting a garden in useable, unused space is vandalism as well as trespassing. These restrictions and controls on our lives are so entrenched that most of us cannot see them. In reality, the choices available to us are limited to what color phone we buy, the model of car we drive, the job we work at if we're lucky (not to work, to choose) and the like. Red handcuffs or blue handcuffs. Anything too far outside this culture's mandate is not accepted; non-participation is not a legitimate option.

That's a problem.

If this culture, this way of life, is fundamentally unsustainable, and we are all trapped in it by having to pay for food, rent, etc., how can a sustainable alternative evolve? Really, if we are all forced to work as part of a death machine, with no other viable alternative, where is the possibility for a sustainable future? The answer is obvious: in breaking the rules. Or, to put it more accurately, breaking the *ridiculously insane* rules.

What We're Up Against

As I outlined earlier, cultures are shaped by their food and their relationship to the land. Civilization supports itself through monocultural farming and acts as a monoculture itself. Any other culture, any other sustainable way of life, is not tolerated. It must be eliminated or assimilated. This is what happened and is still happening to Native Americans and all other groups of indigenous people everywhere. Even if they are not actively resisting civilization, humans living outside of this culture's mandate are not allowed. Individuals, yes (lone mountain men can get away with being lone mountain men), but actual thriving communities, not so much. Back-to-the-land religious communities can get by because they still play by the rules, paying for land, taxes and so on, and operate on a Judeo-Christian, agricultural mandate similar to this culture's. If we want to create something healthy, a viable alternative to the dominant culture, it's going to be tricky. We're going to have to be smart about it, as the system is designed in fundamental ways to prevent this from happening. Let's talk about some obstacles and strategies.

The Land

By now, many of the most inhabitable places on the planet have had cities built over them. I'm thinking of fertile river valleys and the like (most cities are built at the mouth of or alongside a river). These areas once supported large populations of indigenous humans and non-humans (food). They are the areas one would presumably be "walking away" from. What this means is that, in many areas, the places where one could potentially live outside of the system are far more marginal than those that indigenous people inhabited. Where I live, on Vancouver Island, people traditionally had their villages at or near the mouths of abundant salmon-bearing rivers.

Much of inland Vancouver Island was totally uninhabited by humans, being more rugged and mountainous, away from the abundant seashore—hardly as easy a place to get by in as the coast. These days, all of those abundant lowlands are populated and privately owned, making the less abundant, rugged areas the only option.

The bison herds that supported traditional cultures on the Great Plains are gone, much of the topsoil washed away. The Eastern woodlands have lost their native chestnuts to blight, the Eastern cod overfished to oblivion. We will be learning to live in marginalized landscapes. Some will be too toxic (a large area around any nuclear disaster, or possibly any decommissioned nuclear plant, for example).

On the flip side, for a limited time we have all of the collective knowledge of civilization at our fingertips, via the Internet, to learn, for example, how to establish (or re-establish) resilient, appropriate food sources in a given area. Living as an indigenous person on the land now, or in ten, fifty, one hundred years from now, is going to look quite a bit different than it did traditionally.

Learn about the original ecology of where you are living, how the original inhabitants of that place lived, study how things have changed and strategies for adaptation.

Community Sufficiency

This has already been mentioned, but in order to make any moves away from the dominant culture, we need to break our reliance on it. That means having the knowledge and ability to provide ourselves food, water, shelter, health care, hygiene, defense, entertainment, clothing, fuel, etc.

Learning practical skills is absolutely essential. Everyone doesn't have to learn everything, that's what community is for.

In the present, breaking our bonds with this culture also means simply being frugal, avoiding choices that perpetuate our own slavery. This could mean dumpster diving, gardening, getting clothes from thrift stores and tools from garage sales, scavenging roadkill or harvesting wild greens. Choices that move us away from the monetary economy and coincidentally connect us to something healthy.

Momentum

Many feel that all they have to do is quit their job, hit the road (or trail) and they will be wild and free, living the dream. After a whole life of conditioning to respond to bells and whistles, though (first with school, then work), most people fall flat on their faces when they no longer have that structure in their lives.

It is quite sad, but I see it illustrated whenever I hear someone complain that they've been out of work too long, that they're bored.

Bored? Of being free to live and be alive?

This is one of the worst ways we have been degraded: stripped of the ability to thrive in unstructured time, also known as living.

Imagine that everyone who dropped out of the system put as much work into building something new and healthy, or halting the destruction, as those in the system put into their 9–5 jobs! Well, working that much is probably unsustainable by nature, and we'd end up chopping down forests and damming rivers just trying to occupy ourselves, but do you see what I'm getting at? Industrial society has an incredible momentum; all you need do is plug in, use whatever drugs keep you functional (caffeine, sugar, SSRIs), and you don't really need to think. It's like jumping into a river: it's moving in one direction and it carries you that way. There is the collective momentum of over seven billion people—most all of humanity. Step out of the system and "poof," the momentum is gone.

Living in unstructured time, or creating one's own structure, can be incredibly difficult and depressing for many. For those that don't naturally have strong internal motivation, it means somehow cultivating it or creating healthy structures to keep yourself focused and motivated. This might sound like a silly issue to even mention, but it is incredibly huge, there's a whole genre of literature on it: "Self Help" (which I kind of hope this book isn't classified as).

Set goals. Draw strength and motivation from the land friends lovers songs stars food water spirit.

While industrial society has the collective momentum of nearly seven billion humans, wild aliveness has the collective momentum of everything else in the universe. Tap into that.

Squatting: Creating Autonomous Zones

When we talk about breaking out of the system and creating something new that can grow through the cracks, a big part of this is learning how to provide food and shelter for ourselves. Or, at the least, not being indentured to the system for such "privileges." Autonomy.

One strategy toward this end, that seems to get shrugged off all too often as unrealistic, is squatting. Most people with an inclination towards living on the land have thought about it, some have tried it, most haven't. I see squatting (living in a space without paying for the "right" to do so) as an amazing strategy. There is huge potential in it for people to create autonomous spaces in which people can learn physical, social and community-building skills that under normal circumstances cannot be learned within the confines of the system, all the while actually building something outside of it.

My experiences with squatting have been overall quite

positive, more than I can say for some friends involved in "legitimate" land projects. Squatting land with a group of people can be a way of learning some very hard social skills, working through one's own baggage and seeing how group dynamics can and can't work. All of these lessons are free of monetary charge to the squatter, and if the project fails, as many land or housing projects do regardless of their legality, there will probably be a much smaller load of hard feelings between the participants than if they were all deeply intertwined financially. Also, in the event of a hard crash, no one is going to kick you off; the illusions of ownership will have been washed away, leaving you with the same level of rights as a "legitimate" landowner.

Here are a few things to keep in mind when looking for a piece of land to squat.

- Is it privately owned, park, national forest, crown or Bureau of Land Management land? Squatting in a park may be attractive, and may work out quite well, but if a park official finds you out, they have procedures to follow, which include removing you. A private landowner has no direct higher-ups to answer to, and can therefore be an understanding human if they choose to; they can also be brutally unsympathetic. Vacant city lots and other land that has been repossessed by banks are becoming more and more plentiful in some areas and is another viable option.

- Remoteness has advantages and disadvantages. You will be much less likely to get found out. You will also be more socially isolated. Don't underestimate how significant this is; humans are social creatures, especially healthy ones.

- If it's not remote, who are the neighbors? Will they be supportive? If not, will you be able to keep a low profile?

- Be stealthy, keep things clean. Be careful who you allow into your space, but not paranoid.

Squatting is also a viable approach to urban living. I know people that have lived for over a year in an empty old house, slated to be demolished, that still had electricity. Many American cities have a growing phenomenon of vacancy. In places like Detroit, growing numbers of people are taking advantage of large amounts of vacant lots and abandoned homes by moving in and starting gardens.

What are the drawbacks? The most significant one is that families with children may think twice about squatting; it could land them in trouble with social services and jeopardize their ability to keep their children. It's something worth considering, something that I suspect will change with the political climate in the coming years as Western countries adapt to a lower standard of living and a lot more people become squatters.

A feeling of uncertainty and inability to sink into longer-term projects can also be a problem, since one could be evicted any time. Of course, over the five years I spent squatting in one place, all of my friends that rent were shuffling around from one home to another, often evicted with a month's notice, so I suppose this is nothing out of the ordinary. Live every day to the fullest; give as much to the project as makes sense; be intelligent but don't hold back if you've found a good situation.

For those with the financial means, buying land and creating a more legitimate autonomous zone is of course an option. I'm guessing you've thought of it before? By all means, if you have the desire and the means, make your space more secure.

Community

If we want to create something viable, a real alternative to the dominant culture, it needs to fulfill our inherent needs for community. This is huge. For a healthy community to evolve, the people it is made up of need to be healthy (you can see what I mean by "this is huge"), they need to be able to communicate, to have solid, long-standing, long-lasting bonds, and share a collective sense of meaning and purpose. They need to be able to deal with abusive behavior coming from within and without. To live outside the system's swift current and have solid community is something to aspire towards, something to work at and cultivate.

Don't Walk Away!

Considering one really can't get away from the effects of civilization, perhaps a wiser strategy would be to connect to the land, build community and autonomy, wherever you are, wherever you can, wherever makes sense. That could be in the Yukon wilderness, a rural area on the edge of a small city, or the vacant neighborhoods of a collapsing city.

If everyone disenchanted with this culture decided to wander off into the lonesome wilderness, it would have absolutely no effect on its workings. The back-to-the-land communities of the '60s and '70s may provide an illustration of this: a movement that was solid and strong in urban centers scattered into the countryside and gently faded away in dysfunctional utopian communities.

I think the most strategic place to be is on the fringes of this culture, in rural areas and at the edges of cities and towns. There one can interact with both civilization and wildness, dancing back and forth between both, feeding off the mass human energy and non-human energy. For those who feel called, there is important work to be done in the cities and in the wild blue yonder.

What we need is to build autonomous spaces, to create havens where the tools and skills we are going to need can be developed, and this can happen anywhere. Actually, it needs to be happening *everywhere*.

CHAPTER 6

Reflections at the End
of the World

S OMETIMES I THINK about the end of the world. Everyone
does. For a while I thought peak oil and climate change
together would bring a swift collapse to civilization. Without petroleum-based fertilizers, degraded farmlands and cli-
matic shifts would quickly bring the human population to a
sane level, put an end to the project of industrial civilization
and basically force humans to exist sustainably. I have come
across many who believe a great shift in consciousness is imminent, based on the prophecies of ancient Mayan civilization
and other cultures around the world. What that shift means
or how it might take shape (and somehow stop the wheels of
destruction) varies from person to person, but that its time has
come is certain. Most people who are aware of what is going
on here, and especially those who are opposed to it, have a tendency to see an apocalypse on the horizon. Of course Chris-
tians have their end times prophecies as well, and one could
argue they are working hard to fulfill them.

Why do we see an end coming? Because picturing a future
without a massive jolt to rearrange this culture horrifies us?

Because we can use these scenarios of doom and mass enlight-enment as an easy way out of the incredibly complex mess we were born into—this world?

"Apocalypse" has a double meaning, of course. On the one hand it implies tragedy, massive cataclysmic changes, death, disease, loss. On the other, it implies rebirth, which is actually closer to the original meaning of the word (it stems from a Greek word meaning "lifting the veil" or "revelation"). Most of us who see a great change on the horizon picture whatever lies beyond it as better than what came before. If you are a Christian that might mean chilling with JC in a New Age, if you are a 2012-er that might mean flying around tasting color and checking out crystals in different dimensions; if you are a "primitivist" that might mean living intimately with and heal-ing the land and people, becoming rooted.

We have to wonder, though—have people been certain the end is "really" coming for as long as civilization has ex-isted? Is something really going to give in our lives? Is it wise to wait for these great changes to happen for us, changes that rely on forces outside ourselves? Or is all this a reaction to a desperate situation? I don't doubt the reality of peak oil, cli-mate change and general ecological annihilation as serious problems facing civilization and life on Earth (not peak oil; I don't think any non-humans are too worried about less emis-sions), but will they bring some kind of apocalypse? I don't know. Nobody knows. There are a few things I do know, how-ever, and they have helped my thoughts on all of this continu-ally evolve.

I grew up near a town that was once inhabited by indig-enous people, called the Pentlatch. There are none of them left to tell their story, so all I have heard is shreds of what European colonists said about them. All I really know about the Pentlatch is that their world ended when colonists arrived. Smallpox hit, bodies were piled in their villages as the dead outnumbered the living. Whites raped the women and girls, introduced alcohol, committed massacres, forced them from their homes and land. Like I said, there are no more Pentlatch people, they were eradicated. Now a town of 80,000 sits on their homeland and most of its inhabitants have never heard the word Pentlatch.

I know that when the colonists arrived the world ended for the massive herds of bison on the Great Plains. Before European contact an estimated 30 million bison were living on the massive prairies. Upon arrival colonists set out on a mission to completely eradicate these herds. The US government had an explicit policy to eliminate the bison so that hostile native cultures would be starved to death, or forced to take up farming. "A bison dead means a Indian dead," was the slogan. Between 1871 and 1875, four million bison were killed; 1.4 million skins were shipped from Dodge City, Kansas, merely one trade center. Most of the millions of bison killed during these years were left to rot. By 1889 there were less than 2,000 bison in North America. Their world ended, and the cultures that depended on them, their worlds ended too.

In the summer of 2010, the world ended for vast areas of the Gulf of Mexico, as unimaginable amounts of crude oil and methane spewed into it, up to a hundred thousand barrels a day for three months. Nearly a million gallons of the toxic oil dispersant Corexit (evidently far more toxic than the crude itself) was dumped to keep the oil under water (out of sight, out of mind) and inadvertently break it down into the food chain more rapidly. The Deepwater Horizon oil well, where all of this occurred, is just one of thousands in the Gulf of Mexico alone.

Privilege and Doom

So it would seem that for many human and non-human communities, the world has already ended. Still, knowing this, people always talk about "the end" in the future tense.

Often during conversations about "the crash," people tend to think the unthinkable will happen. A police state will ensue, gangs of looters will develop, desperately plundering whatever food, water and weapons they can get their hands on, people will be starving and freaking out. I'm not going to deny that these aren't real possibilities, but when we talk about a hard crash, what we are really talking about is transitioning to a Third World lifestyle, rapidly. *Most of the world is already living like this*, and while many people are suffering, starving and quarrelling in these places, people are also just carrying on with life.

It's kind of like the argument for police: "If we didn't have cops we'd all be killing one another!"

Not true. If we didn't have cops, communities would evolve and enforce their own boundaries and taboos. If someone was raped, the community would respond by finding the person who committed that rape and holding them accountable. Perhaps in some communities this would evolve slowly, while in others groups as centralized and corrupt as the police might develop.

The same logic dominates people's thoughts on collapse: "If we don't have food in the stores, gas in our tanks, hot running water, Facebook and ice cream we'll all starve and kill each other." Again, in reality, wherever communities exist they will do what they can to organize and distribute whatever food there is among the people, treat the sick, figure out water and protect themselves from aggressive elements. The infrastructure in most areas of the developed world is set up to make this transition very difficult, as is the social structure (most people do not live in what one could call a functional community). Still, if the rest of the world is doing it, why are rich Westerners so afraid?

If you really want to prepare for the crash, start building community and autonomy. Live somewhere you want to be for a long time. Incorporate non-humans into your community, ones that you can eat and keep yourself warm with. Don't be afraid, and don't expect a great and glorious new tomorrow.

The Ghost Dance

In the summer of 1889, on the western plains of America, indigenous peoples were facing an impossibly difficult, catastrophic reality. Disease brought from European newcomers had ravaged their people, the bison herds that they traditionally depended on had been all but exterminated and white settlers, backed by the United States military, were relentlessly appropriating their lands. Many had been forcibly relocated to reserves where they were expected to farm and send their children to boarding school—become white.

After years of fighting back, the cultures of the plains were growing weak and weary, their numbers dropping to battle, massacre, starvation and disease. They were coming up against a juggernaut—civilization—that had its eyes on their land and was not going to stop. It was against this backdrop that a religious movement called the Ghost Dance appeared.

The Ghost Dance was a new religion blending aspects of Christianity and traditional spirituality. It was born through the visions of a Paiute man named Wovoka. Wovoka had received a vision in which God took him to a place where his Paiute ancestors were enjoying life, living in the old ways in peace with one another, in a land with plenty of game to hunt. They sang, danced, and no whites were there to bother them. God instructed Wovoka to teach his people a dance, and told him that if they performed the dance in five-day intervals at the appropriate times, they would hasten a new era of peace and prosperity and the encroachment of the whites would be halted. Indeed, the prophecy told that the whites would turn into little wooden figurines or disappear.

The Ghost Dance quickly swept across the American West, many tribes dancing at the appropriate intervals to fulfill the prophecy of a new age, a "renewed Earth" in which "all evil is washed away." Having been displaced from their lands onto small, marginal reservations and facing starvation, the Ghost Dance provided the people of the plains hope.

White authorities were disturbed by this new movement. Even though it was pacifistic, it felt dangerous and unsettling to them. Perhaps they feared there was truth to the prophecy, that they would all disappear if the dancing continued unchecked. Or, perhaps, having brought many of these tribes nearly to the brink of extinction, they simply despised everything "Indian" and thought these people should have fallen silent and given up already.

On the Lakota reservations of South Dakota, Ghost Dancing was outlawed. Leaders were punished, yet the ritual persisted. By December of 1890, thousands of troops were called in to get things under control. The situation escalated as Lakota Ghost Dancers continued their ritual and the military presence grew more anxious and impatient. The situation culminated in the now-infamous massacre at Wounded Knee that winter. A group of Lakota, camping at Wounded Knee, were approached by a group of US soldiers. Some of the warriors brought out their old rifles in defense, and a short skirmish turned quickly into mass murder. The US military killed 157 Lakota, most of whom were unarmed women and children, and piled their bodies in a mass grave.

Twenty US soldiers received medals of honor for their actions.

The Ghost Dance movement quietly disappeared.

This story tragically illustrates the brutality inherent to colonization. There are also difficult lessons to take from it. Prophecies can be dangerous. Waiting for a magical transition to a great and glorious new tomorrow is often a reaction to a desperate situation. A reaction that does nothing to improve that situation, a reaction that ignores reality, awful as it may be, in favor of fantasy.

No End in Sight

Every day the world is ending, or has long since ended, for many communities. There isn't a great big finale coming—it's here. It's been here for a long time, and there isn't going to be an end to it in our lives. Hoping for an ideal future, a sudden change that stops it all, is not real, that's not what's going on here. Our lifetimes, if we are not sedated, are going to be filled with loss and struggle, and when we embrace that we can move through it with more strength and determination. The "end" is slow, continual, messy and real.

We don't need to wait for any Armageddon, though big waves and rifts will likely come—the world is already falling apart around us. For many the world has fallen apart.

Every day is the most beautiful day ever, as well as the saddest.

CHAPTER 7

On Being White

Everywhere the white man goes
he brings misery
all throughout history,
look it up.
« Dead Prez »

WHEN I WAS 18, I saw a mask. I was traveling by my-self in Northwest Mexico, in a small town nestled in the mountains of Chihuahua on traditional Raramuri land. Raramuri inhabit the Sierra Madre of Chihuahua, a beautiful mountain range where they have taken refuge from civiliza-tion's encroachment for many centuries, while still practicing a semi-traditional way of life. Inhabiting caves, cliff overhangs and cabins built from pine logs and stone, Raramuri subsist by growing corn and beans, hunting wild game or living as nomadic herders. In the small town's general store, I saw the Raramuri mask—it was a pale face carved from wood with a scraggly brown beard made from some wooly hair. Beside the mask was a written description of its meaning that said: "This is the white man. The hairs on his face represent all of the pain, suffering and misery in the world."

Raramuri don't grow much facial hair.

Walking on dirt roads and trails through the country, I re-member coming across the dwellings and gardens of Raramuri families, seeing them dart behind corn or into the pines when they realized a white person was walking by. I was the enemy.

I left that place wishing I belonged somewhere like they did, wishing I wasn't just another white tourist that belonged to nowhere, though I understood, respected and even admired their disdain for what my ancestry represented to them. I went back home to get to work.

White Europeans first came to the Northwest coast, my home, just over 200 years ago. They found thriving indigenous communities here that had been living sustainably forever. They found oceans and rivers teeming with life, forests of supernaturally enormous cedar, spruce and hemlock. Through the eyes of the indigenous cultures living here and the land itself, they must have appeared to be coming from hell, bringing nothing but misery, determined from the beginning to turn this land into part of the hell from whence they came.

Two hundred years into this story—history—European colonists vastly outnumber indigenous inhabitants here. Almost all of the original inhabitants (rain forests, salmon, humans) have been degraded, razed or pushed back into corners at the hands of the newcomers. So much so that the colonizers are often no longer aware that anything existed here before them—that a rainforest lived where the Wal-Mart parking lot sits, that people had to be killed or assimilated and their cultures destroyed in order to take the land from them, that it wasn't simply vacant when colonists arrived. Many of us in this colonial culture don't understand that civilization is fighting an ongoing war on the land and indigenous people. Our own colonization runs so deep that present victims aren't recognized as sentient.

Those that weren't physically killed are killed in other ways, methodically, until they fit into their place in the white man's world—if they have one. From the perspective of this land and the indigenous plants and animals living here, I am sure that European colonists look like demons. In two centuries, only the blink of an eye to the cultures that existed here for thousands of years, they have waged a ruthless war on this land, bringing it to an apocalyptic state.

This is my heritage.

When Europeans began their invasion into North America, European civilization was on the brink of collapse. Their homeland was plagued by famine, overpopulation, warfare and, of course, plagues. Civilization had eliminated any kind of freedom to live outside of its hierarchy. "Poaching" (harvesting food from the forest) was punished with death. Life for the common person was nasty, brutish and short. It was, comparatively, hell, and spawned the violent conquistadors that pillaged much of North America.

When these explorers encountered the relatively pristine land and sustainable cultures of Turtle Island, instead of thinking they had found something beautiful, a better way of life, they appear to have worked as fast as possible to degrade what was here and turn it into another overpopulated waste of human depravity. This hasn't stopped, only accelerated. Technological advancements have allowed us to make hell a much more awful place every day.

But what is the "white man" possessed by? Where does the sick heart of this culture come from? When Earth-loving people talk about civilization being destructive, we often talk as though it were some kind of accident or mistake, that deep down everyone is a good person and the system is just out of control. We talk about how civilization is just a house of cards, a very vulnerable system that could fall easily from any number of glitches (grid-crash, changes in the climate, peak oil, etc.). The reality is that ecological destruction, genocide and economic warfare are murder. This system is not some abstract entity working on its own, it is a massive movement of people possessed by a powerful force, working collectively to an end, whether or not they are conscious of what that end really means. Violence, oppression and destruction are not accidental glitches in the system, they are its mode of operation, business as usual.

On one hand, race has nothing to do with this destructiveness; civilization is perpetuated by many far-flung cultural groups. But my story, and the story of North America, is one dominated by horrible destruction wrought by the European colonists, who happen to currently be at the top of this culture's pyramid. My story is intertwined with the story of colonization.

I am a young white male (blonde hair, blue eyes, even), born into a lineage of colonizers, disgusted with what my forefathers did here and what continues all around me. As a white male, how do I reconcile myself to this?

I begin by separating my identity from the white man. That's not me. I shared the opening quote of this piece with a friend recently (*everywhere the white man goes he brings misery...*). She was put off by it. She said it seemed like too much of a blanket statement. I disagreed. I interpret it as meaning that when one says "everywhere the white man goes," they are referring to European (white), patriarchal (man), colonizers (goes), who are going somewhere to exploit, instead of staying in their homeland. In this context, it's absolutely true, they do always bring misery. She agreed.

When the first European boats arrived on this coast, the people here were shocked by something that we often don't consider strange: those on board the boats were all *men*—they had no families, they had no wives or children with them, and they had no home. In the view of the people here they were lost, crazed, hungry ghosts. It is a really fascinating phenomenon: look at the gold rushes, the mining, the oil fields, the military—it's often single men on the front lines, men who don't have families (or have left them behind) and don't have a home, a sense of place.

I don't identify with the white man's world, the trajectory set forth by my recent predecessors. I don't accept that my destiny as a white male is to be an oppressor. I was born into this storm, I didn't make it, and I will not perpetuate it. I didn't decide to invade anyone's land, to clear the forests and kill the rivers. None of this is my doing. I was born into a world that had been toxified, where I am considered free, but only free to live inside the colonial system, which requires me to join or support the ongoing war against life in order to pay rent and have food. This is not freedom.

If I look back, my ancestors—nomadic reindeer hunter-herders in Scandinavia and acorn-gathering fisher people in the British Isles—were living sustainably not long ago (a thousand years really isn't that long in the bigger story) and were swept into this culture. So were yours. The process of assimilation that is so recent (and ongoing) in North America happened long enough ago to my ancestors that there is no memory of it, there are no stories. My story was stolen, and I find myself connecting to a land base that I have no stories from, where I have no elders to teach me about life and where I live. I have no roots here, they are only just starting to dig in after living my life so far in place.

Being white in North America means being somewhat lost.

Again, imperialism and colonialism are obviously perpetuated by many groups that aren't of European descent; the problem of civilization is much larger than any one ethnic group's contribution. Still, white male capitalists are at the top of the pyramid of industrial civilization right now, and have the bloodiest track record of anyone. My skin color allows me to blend in and maneuver seamlessly in a racist culture.

For instance, if I were black, people would see me walking onto the trail that leads to my home in the woods (I live in a predominantly white area) and say, "Hey, look at that black guy going into the woods!" and likely be concerned. As it is, they often don't even see me, my pale skin acts as racist camouflage. If I were of Haida ancestry, people wouldn't pick me up hitchhiking nearly as much, because they would think I was a "drunk Indian" (the number of people that have told me this is astounding).

The Relevance of Race

"It's the 21st century, race really isn't a relevant issue any more." Have you ever heard this kind of comment? Have you even thought it? It's a common sentiment among white privileged Westerners; it is also completely out of touch with reality.

Twenty-one percent of the prison population in Canada is made up of indigenous people. Four percent of the general Canadian population are indigenous people. People of African ancestry make up 40 percent of the prison population in the United States while they make up only 12 percent of the general population. Statistics regarding poverty along racial lines follow the same trend. This is called systemic racism; Western society is based on it. Civilization has always seen itself as superior and those on the outside of it as savages and degenerates to be eliminated or assimilated as subordinate workers. The currently dominant white, European-driven civilization sees non-whites as "those degenerates," and systematically rigs the cards against them. This is not up for debate, it is irrefutable. If anyone finds this difficult to understand or accept, that speaks volumes about where they are in relation to the center of power.

The question for me is, really, how did we get so messed up? How did European colonizers come to be? How did this Earth produce a people who heartlessly exterminated the bison, the salmon, all of the ancient forests, and have moved on to killing whole oceans, a whole planet nearly? People who massacred whole villages of unarmed Native families, pretending nothing ever happened there, create misogynist pornography to educate their youth on sexuality and on and on.

Perhaps the answer to that question is obvious: the Earth didn't produce the white male oppressor, the white male oppressor did. Civilization did. Just as whole cultures are broken and assimilated into this one, every child must be broken. Every school feeds the same poison as the residential schools that stripped Native youth of their identity. The poison at the core of this culture is passed on, we aren't born with it; it is the result and the goal of colonization. *When our goals, views and perception fall in line with the plans of those in power, we have been fully colonized.*

Our Stories

Indigenous people have a clear story—their exploitation and assimilation are right on the surface, their homeland is clear, the perpetrator is extremely obvious. For non-natives things are much more cloudy and confusing. It is easy to identify with our predecessors, the explorers, miners, military officers, movie stars and political heroes that make this culture. Being white means being closer to the center of power. It means getting less harassment from cops, getting jobs easier, fitting into an inherently racist society. This privilege obviously makes it difficult to bother looking at things from another, more challenging perspective. For the most part, people don't. We need to.

Those of us who were born white need to break our identities away from this abusive culture, from our exploitative forefathers. It is common knowledge that someone sexually abused as a child will have a high likelihood of repeating that abusive behavior later in life, that most abusers were abused as children. It is a learned behavior. In order for the cycle of abuse to stop, they must acknowledge and heal from their trauma. They must recognize their abuser as an abuser and go into the memories that may have been intentionally buried.

The training this culture puts its members through is abusive. Breaking a wild creature into a submissive drone is abusive. Genital mutilation—are you circumcised? I am—is abusive. This culture not only abuses people of color, it abuses everyone and every living thing, turning us all into perpetrators against some inferior other.

We need to observe, acknowledge and unlearn the racist conditioning inflicted upon us, along with the privilege inherent to our skin tone. This next statement, though, might be controversial: we cannot and should not try to ignore the privileges that come inherently with our ancestry. Instead, we should acknowledge these privileges and even use them wisely, not in ways that perpetuate inequality, but to navigate our way towards a society that is truly tolerant, healthy and completely intolerant of racism, empire and genocide.

Beneath the layers of poisonous miseducation, we are all indigenous creatures, uprooted and displaced.

CHAPTER 8

Veganism or
Radical Sustainability?
Tough Questions about Diet

V EGANISM IS OFTEN hailed as an obvious answer to the
global food crisis, the most sustainable and natural diet
for human societies—an alternative to the misery of industrial
feedlots. I'm not vegan. I have been, as have nearly all of my
friends, and the same force that drew me briefly to a plant-
based diet and vegan ethics has continued to guide me as I
connect more deeply with non-human animals. At one time I
believed veganism was a solution to many of the world's problems; I no longer do. I no longer believe that a vegan diet is
even a healthy way for human creatures to eat. I have seen no
proof of a traditional, healthy, sustainable human culture that
has been vegan. What I do see is that the same concerns, mo-
tivations, loves and passions that guide many toward a vegan
diet are those that also guide me. My purpose here is to show
how vegan ethics are incomplete, not to put people down. My
purpose here is not to further alienate vegans, but rather to
show that there can be a huge depth and love behind the motivation to kill creatures for food, in a way that is healthy and

intelligent—to put vegan ethics on the table and chop them to pieces, see what's really in there and what it's worth.

Radical Sustainability

What do I mean by *radical* sustainability, and how does it relate to veganism? Radical comes from the Latin *radix*—root. Radical sustainability is a kind of sustainability that has deep *roots*. It's not something civilized, colonized (and colonizing) people are coming up with from the distorted vantage point of industrial life, but something that we see when we look to our indigenous heritage, into the land and the big story of who we are. It is something we can look to and see. People existed *here* without killing the land. How did they do it?

I make this distinction between radical and simple sustainability because "sustainability" by itself has become meaningless. People bend it to serve their purpose—every big auto, oil and agricultural corporation claims to have "sustainability" as their primary concern. The word has been killed, it's been made to mean too many things, most of which are never actually sustainable—that is, nourishing or maintaining life.

How does this relate to veganism? To put it simply, if we look at our roots, the life ways of our indigenous ancestors, we don't see anything resembling a vegan diet or way of life. Traditionally, sustainable cultures everywhere have two qualities that exclude them from being vegan: they don't farm and they are omnivores, consuming animals as food be it as insects, eggs, fish or mammals. If we really look, we'll see that vegan ethics do not have deep roots at all.

But wait. Vegan literature claims the opposite, that a plant-based diet is the most natural food for humans, so who is bullshitting here? I'll get to that in a bit.

There are many levels that vegan ethics are built on, but I mostly want to address the two big ones here: that it is the most sustainable method of subsistence; and that it is a biologically appropriate, healthful diet for humans.

Efficient, Not Sustainable

Most of us turn away from animal foods in reaction to factory meat and dairy farming, and with good reason. Industrial feedlots are one of the most horrible creations imaginable, a manifestation of the absolute potential ugliness of the human heart. Make no mistake—I am not a supporter of industrial farming on any level. I am not encouraging anyone to eat factory farmed meat! In fact my critique has evolved to the point where farming in general is questionable.

The simple, obvious reaction to the industrial feedlot system goes like this: People are starving, and animals are suffering horribly so that rich North Americans can feast on toxic meat and dairy. We need to take the grain we are wasting in the feedlots and distribute it to the Third World. We *can* stop world hunger and the senseless immiseration of non-humans! It's so simple!

That is one level to the problem, but falls way short of addressing the root of it. Here is another take: Humans have lived sustainably, like all other creatures, for millennia. The big shift came when we began farming—when we began to transform wild spaces into spaces engineered to produce human food. No longer subject to the same natural laws that govern all life, our population exploded, more wild land was colonized and converted to human production, population grew even more, and so on. We are still in the cycle of domestication, displacement and growth. Veganism does not address this, and actually fits quite perfectly into this cycle of domestication.

If we broaden our concept of sustainability to understand that civilization, agriculture and domestication are inherently unsustainable, then veganism dissolves as any kind of solution.

It is a diet that has evolved with agriculture and the most privileged class of civilization. It does not challenge domestication,
absolutely the most unnatural aspect to our lives, and actually
strongly reinforces it.

I think veganism should be defined as *efficient*, not *sustainable*. This is because within the context of civilization—
which is inherently unsustainable—it is a more efficient way
for humans to live. In fact, I'm sure those at the top of this
culture's pyramid know that it would be more efficient to cut
the cattle out and feed all the grain and soy in their feedlots
straight to the humans and strongly support the endless sea of
vegan literature.

Something very interesting and disturbing on this note re-
vealed itself to me recently; I was reading a book, *The Nutritional Bypass* by David Rowland, which examined the diet of
prison guards to defend the argument that cholesterol doesn't
cause heart disease. Apparently it is common for prison guards
to be fed large amounts of eggs on their shift, the easily assimilated proteins and fatty acids helping them stay alert. It
works, and they are not at any elevated risk for heart disease
whatsoever. What are the inmates fed? Soy in its many mani-
festations, which, because of its high levels of carcinogenic
phytoestrogens, is poisoning them, making them weak and
feeble. One really has to think, who controls all of the dietary
wisdom people in the larger institutions of this world are told?
Could there be parallels between those prisoners, the guards
and us?

A vegan culture would be a culture of domestication. It
would be a culture based on dogma. Instead of living off what
the land offers (gathering, foraging, passively gardening and
hunting plant, animal, insect communities), it would require
that the "proper" food (grains? beans?) be grown.

What is Natural?

By saying that veganism is not a traditional way of life for humans, but is something that has evolved very recently and our bodies are not adapted to, I am contradicting an enormous amount of literature that says the exact opposite. But, really, let's just take a few examples of cultures around the world that lived in balance and were extremely healthy, and see what they ate.

Where I live on Vancouver Island, in the temperate northwest of North America, the Coast Salish people were very healthy. In the early 20th century an American dentist named Weston Price came here to study the indigenous people and their health on a traditional diet. In all of the skulls he examined pre-dating European contact (and civilized foods), incidences of tooth decay were extremely rare to nonexistent. Their diet gave their bodies exactly what they needed to perform complex functions like the re-mineralization of dental enamel (anyone who is vegan very long can appreciate this).

What did they eat? Fish, grease (whale, fish, bear, seal etc.), sea mammals, shellfish, berries, deer and a variety of seasonal plant foods (salmonberry shoots, pacific silverweed rhizomes, etc.). They were extremely healthy people, prizing grease, guts and flesh as their most vital foods. The inhabitants of the North American plains had pemmican as their staple food — dried, pounded bison meat formed into balls with highly saturated animal fat from rendered marrow or intestinal fat — exactly what politically correct nutrition tells us to avoid. And yet these people had no heart disease, tooth decay, cancer, diabetes, osteoporosis or obesity. At this point people say: "But they lived differently! They were more physically active." No doubt, they had to bust their asses sometimes, but what about those month-long feasts in the longhouse? I am pretty positive they did their fair share of just sitting around and feasting, perhaps more than some of us. It is common knowledge among anthropologists that hunter-gatherers work much less than farmers. It is common knowledge, too, that they are healthier than farmers and that they do not destroy their land bases. Industrialized farming, of course, requires almost no direct human contact with the land and little labor, but we still find all sorts of things to busy our bodies.

Traditional human cultures across the world have been omnivorous; there are no examples of an indigenous vegan society. None. When Dr. Price traveled to indigenous cultures across the planet, he found they all prized animal organs and animal fats as their most nourishing, life-giving foods. Even in warm climates, animal foods are loved and celebrated by indigenous people—think Maori, !Kung, Hadza, Mbuti (Pygmy) or indigenous Australian—as essential to life.

But what about the argument that humans have the digestive system and teeth of a herbivore? I'm not sure how many times I have read that, but I am really curious how people came up with it.

Take a mammal of a similar size to us, like deer. They are herbivores; they have a four-chambered stomach for slowly fermenting and digesting cellulose. They regurgitate food that has been partially digested, masticate and then swallow to continue the digestion. They lack upper incisors, and instead have a pad where we have our pearly whites (those teeth you show when you smile). Humans, on the other hand, have a single-chambered stomach that food passes through quite quickly, comparatively, the length of our intestinal tract being relatively similar to that of a raccoon, bear, or other *omnivore*. Humans can thrive on a diet of raw, unadulterated animal foods (meat, fat, organs), but many plant foods contain anti-nutrients (oxalic acid in greens, phytic acid in grains/seeds) or are simply indigestible without some kind of adulteration (cooking, fermenting, etc.).

Cultures that come closest to being total raw foodists also seem to have the highest concentration of animal foods (I am thinking of the Inuit). The reverse is true for those with more of a focus on plant foods (e.g., China). We are biologically omnivores. Sorry, it's pretty much that straightforward. Humans thrive with plant and animal foods, that is what we have evolved to eat and need. There are examples of cultures that existed for thousands of years consuming almost no plant foods and thriving; there aren't any examples of the reverse. In agricultural communities where animal foods are scarce, they have traditionally been coveted and treasured, with every edible part of a creature being used for nourishment.

Biologically Sustainable?

There is a point where veganism's relationship to sustainability (unsustainable) and how suitable it is for the human body (unsuitable) meet: a diet can only be sustainable if a population can sustain itself, physically, from it. As pure vegans, we wouldn't be able to reproduce after one or two (at the very most) generations (I know some of you are wringing your hands and hoping veganism *really* catches on with that thought).

I have a friend who was a hardcore raw food vegan for a couple of years, before which she had been simply vegan. At one point she didn't bleed for six months. Strangely, she began bleeding again soon after eating a bit of dried deer meat. This is extremely common for women on vegan, and especially raw vegan, diets. What happens when a human creature goes on a diet totally contrary to what they are evolved for? They stop ovulating regularly, or completely. If you don't bleed, it means you don't ovulate (unless you're pregnant), which of course means you cannot reproduce. But because this culture has raised us to hate our bodies, and this applies to women and their cycles quite strongly, not bleeding is perceived as good, rather than an obvious sign of deficiency. Not bleeding (or ovulating) for months is thought to be a sign of health. If male-bodied people were bragging about how they hadn't had an erection in months—they were feeling so healthy on the low-fat raw vegan diet—what would that mean? It would mean that something is wrong—in this case, that dietary cholesterol, a precursor to all the human sex hormones and which is found only in animal foods, has become severely deficient.

My friend also experienced more serious, life-threatening health problems as a result of her deficient diet.

A common affliction for long-time, hardcore vegans is pernicious anemia. A diet that is chronically deficient in B-12 eventually causes the body to stop producing a digestive chemical called intrinsic factor. Intrinsic factor is necessary for B-12 absorption. When our bodies stop producing it, they stop for good and the body loses its ability to absorb B-12, an extremely important nutrient. Once the body has gotten to this point of deprivation, there are two options—megadoses of B-12 via injections (or raw liver juice in the old days) or death. B-12 is found primarily in uncooked meat, organs, shellfish and other animal foods. Plant sources of B-12 are not readily absorbed and often even block absorption. I say this because it is a huge issue for vegans, but a total non-issue for anyone that is omnivorous (especially if they eat raw meat). We have evolved to be omnivorous.

Ethics

"I would only eat meat if I killed it myself!"

This statement is one I have heard countless times from vegetarians and vegans. I often think: Have you ever cleared a forest? Have you ploughed a field—taking the homes and lives of countless wild and feral creatures? While listening to your iPod, because that's what they do? Have you ever driven a massive combine harvester over an endless field of soy lit by your tractor's headlights in the middle of the night? Have you stolen food from exotic places?

Why is it okay to be alienated from some foods and the pain associated with their harvest, but not others?

No Roots, No Easy Answers

It isn't surprising that we are confused, that we really don't know what to eat or how to live. We are coming from a place of complete rootlessness, reared by a culture that eradicates traditional knowledge. Veganism is the child of this situation. Born in the storm of civilization, it has no roots and only makes sense in the context of this confusing culture.

So how do we live?

I have no easy answer, not for myself, not for others. Factory farming is a tragedy, the whole industrial food system is too. Agriculture itself is unsustainable and so, by association, is veganism. We need to learn how to live in balance with what our land bases want to give us — to "live in the hands of the gods," as Daniel Quinn put it. This is how all creatures live, it is the way of life, but how do we realistically get there? Seven billion people cannot live as forager-hunter-gardeners. But then again, seven billion people cannot live under industrial agriculture without killing the planet (and themselves), so that is a moot point. Like all other creatures, if we weren't farming, our land base would determine our population.

Really, there are no easy answers. And that's exactly what veganism can be: something that makes us stop thinking and questioning, something that seems attainable because it plays into the plans of the system. I do not propose we all go back to hunting and gathering, I have no proposition but for us to look at these hard truths, acknowledge them and see where they lead.

There is something beyond veganism, beyond a diet of domestication and dogma. A place-based diet. A diet based on relationship, on the realness of taking plant and animal life, for the greater good of all living things. Talk to the land.

CHAPTER 9

Something in the Rain

We hear there is a substance and it's called plutonium... We don't
know how it is made. We hear the substance uranium is used. We
know it is radioactive... We have seen the photographs of women
and children deformed from radiation. The substance plutonium
becomes interesting to us when we read that certain parts of the
building where it is manufactured have leaks. We don't really
know what this means, if it is like the leak in our roofs, or the
water pipe in the backyard, or if it is a simple word for a process
beyond our comprehension. But we know the word "leak" indicates
error and there is no room for error in the handling of this
substance... All that we know in the business of living
eludes us in this instant.

« Susan Griffin, *Woman and Nature* »

IN THE SPRING OF 2011, we took one of our 50-gallon rain
barrels inside, and covered the others left outdoors. We
heard the rain was going to be coming with poison in it. Not
much, not enough to see, taste, smell or get sick from right
away, but that nobody really knows for sure. An accident happened across the Pacific, a massive tsunami tore apart towns
and cities on Japan's east coast, leading to the meltdown of
several nuclear reactors. People in Japan no doubt were immediately affected by this, but wind currents luckily swept
much of the radioactive cloud billowing out of this disaster
to sea. Colossal amounts of radioactive fallout entered the

atmosphere and traveled around the Pacific Rim, coming back to ocean and earth across the whole planet, though higher concentrations fell in the rain along the western shores of North America.

See, where I live, we drink the rain. Everyone drinks the rain in one form or another, but we collect it ourselves and drink it directly, right after it pours from the sky. We don't have a well or plumbing, so this was a huge deal. I remember my intimate and beautiful relationship with the rain changing for the first time; instead of seeing the rain as a benevolent cleanser, I feared it.

One night as I lay in bed I listened to it beating down on our tin roof, rain that we drink, that the plants and animals we eat and love drink, and there was a sinking feeling in my gut. After reading that Vancouver rainwater had 100 times the allowable level of radioactive iodine, that a public notice had been issued on Haida Gwaii (just upwind from us) warning people that rainwater was no longer "suitable for human consumption," I woke up one morning and took down all of the traps I had set, not wanting to kill anything I wasn't completely excited about eating. I felt incredibly sad.

I continued working in the garden with mixed feelings, asking myself, "Is this all poison that we're going to be eating now?" I continued eating wild greens with mixed feelings; breathing, touching, every physical interaction with the environment, with mixed feelings.

In the course of talking to people about the nuclear disaster (supposedly the worst industrial disaster in the history of the human race), reactions ranged from: "I don't care. I haven't bothered to find anything out about it," to "The world is already screwed isn't it?" to covering their garden beds with plastic in an attempt to keep soil from being contaminated. I'm still processing it. As I write this, nearly a year after the massive tsunami tore apart several nuclear reactors in the coastal Japanese town of Fukushima, radioactive debris washes up on the West Coast. People in Japan are getting sick. The Japanese news anchor who ate produce from the Fukushima region on television to prove it was safe has died from cancer.

The scale of these disasters, the scale of how destructive this culture's mechanisms are, is sometimes beyond our ability to mentally cope with or even grasp. There are 55 active nuclear reactors in Japan alone. When a couple of these went into a meltdown process that lasted nearly a year, the humans that erected them had no idea how to stop it. They pumped ocean water into the reactors and flew helicopters around scooping water out of lakes and dropping it on them like they were getting their directions from local preschoolers (no disrespect to young readers, I've just seen how you pour water on sandcastles and stuff). Their mistakes threaten all life; the technology to create these disasters has been developed, the technology to stop them hasn't.

When the disaster first began, I had a breakdown. I had spent an hour or so reading some of the latest on the developing nightmare across the ocean, reading about levels of cesium in milk, spinach, strawberries and rainwater on this side of the ocean. About "worse than Chernobyl," about how many reactors there are in the world, how long this might go on for. I wished I never had to hear the word cesium again during this life.

My main source of sanity, physical intercourse with a living world, had been tainted.

On the bike ride home I started losing control of my body, felt like my mind was crushing in on itself under the weight of grief. I got home and curled up in a ball to wait it out till the morning—sometimes the weight of this world feels unbearable.

I heard one person say that Fukushima was that famous coastal city where innocent, beautiful dolphins have been brutally killed en masse for human food—that perhaps this was simply karma punishing those insensate people for their crimes against the dolphins. Why is it that karma only seems to be capable of punishing the poorest humans and non-humans? There is no logic to this karma people speak of that always punishes the poorest and leaves the perpetrators (CEOs, politicians, etc.) unscathed. If there is a higher power behind these ongoing atrocities of industrial society, it appears to be a racist, classist, sexist and speciesist power that has a hard time extending karmic justice to the rich and powerful.

It's a bit of a mind game. Like I said above, radioactivity is tasteless, colorless, odorless, so we can choose to ignore it and maybe that would be wiser. Survivalists and others deeply concerned were locking themselves indoors, taping up the cracks around their windows, and stockpiling pre-"3/11" (that's March 11, 2011) food, water, medicine, toilet paper, etc., or leaving for the Southern Hemisphere where winds were not carrying the fallout. Perhaps they are crazy, or perhaps they actually understand what was going on, I have no idea. Though I would lean more in the direction of them being crazy.

All of these protective measures are only available to extremely privileged humans. Deer and rabbits will continue drinking rainwater in puddles and streams, eating fresh grasses and lichen and being drenched in rain. Those humans at the bottom of this culture's hierarchy are still eating whatever they can, drinking whatever water is available, getting drenched in rain, possibly unaware anything is different. As I said above, there are many survivalists who believe they will come out of this disaster unscathed by completely physically disconnecting from the Earth until it is over, and the soil and water are somehow decontaminated. This seems impossible and futile to me, not worth it.

I wonder, how much are people willing to disconnect from the land in order to survive? I am asking from the perspective of someone who loves the land like family, like a lover, like everything that matters. And my answer, for myself, is that in order to be sane and feel alive, I need to touch the land. I need to taste it. I need our bodies to mix.

On the opposite side of this spectrum, standing 180 degrees from me, is Stephen Hawking. Hawking, often hailed as the smartest person alive, has made headlines in recent years by advocating that "mankind" must relocate to outer space in the next hundred years or go extinct. It is absolutely unfathomable to me that anyone would see a life in a biodome, life in an artificially created environment, as worth pursuing. Then I realized that Stephen Hawking cannot move, speak or have any sensual relationship with the land. I am not putting down or judging Mr. Hawking, not by any stretch, just making an observation: he lives very directly as part human, part machine. It makes sense that someone whose identity and survival are so explicitly linked to technology would see life in a machine as a viable option.

I would prefer dying on the Earth.

What I'm talking about here goes beyond any one specific disaster of course. The general state of the Earth right now is that of decline. At this point, connecting to our land bases — rewilding — can feel somewhat like making friends with a dying person. Falling in love with something that is disappearing or, more accurately, under constant threat and siege.

How do we deal with this? How do we continue at all when the world is a double-edged sword, when without genuine, raw connection to wild nature we, as creatures, go insane.

Yet, if we open ourselves up to that connection, we are taking on the reality of how pain-filled this world is. We become part of that pain, realizing our role in it.

It gets worse all the time. If we want to continue, we just have to deal with it; to say, "Okay, you've added another thing to the load, another hitch to this game." Not to accept it, because it is unacceptable, but to have the strength to carry on. I continue eating deer and dandelions, tending and harvesting from a garden, relating intimately with the land—because I have to.

I have thought once or twice, in moments of desperation, about giving up entirely. At those moments I sometimes remember a quote from an old native warrior named Chiksika: *"When an Indian is killed, it is a great loss which leaves a gap in our people and a sorrow in our heart; when a white is killed three or four others step up to take his place and there is no end to it."*

I am not a Native American; I am white. Maybe this quote can apply to me because in my mind I change the word "Indian," to "one who moves with the land," or "one who resists," and "white" (since I am) to "one who follows orders," or "one who moves against the land." There are precious few humans that hear the screams of the Earth, who hold onto the forgotten memory that they are creatures that aren't following their orders, are trying to live in a good way or actively resisting. We need to preserve our troops.

Living in a wounded world is nothing new. It is something we are going to have to work with, another layer to the challenge that confronts us.

CHAPTER 10

Succession

"I maintain that chaos is the future and beyond it lies freedom!
Confusion is next, and next after that is the truth!"
« Thurston Moore »

O NE OF THE MOST interesting things about living in the
same place throughout one's life is watching the land
change. For me this has mostly meant watching whole forests being cleared for strip malls and subdivisions; "interesting" barely begins to do full justice. The more subtle changes of
ever-shifting, never stagnant nature are more what I am talking about, or those situations where the land has been stripped
bare but allowed to regrow, or perhaps the cement is giving in
to new growth.

There's a spot I remember going past on the school bus as
a child, staring out the window at countless baby cottonwood
seedlings coming up in a clearing—these are now big, strong
cottonwood trees in the full vigor of young adulthood that I
have gone and harvested sheets of bark for baskets from, and
who others have been cutting for firewood.

There was a big old maple tree that I once tapped for syrup
making. When I drilled into the tree with my old hand-crank
drill and sap started gushing out of the small wound, I thought
I had stepped in dog poo; I could suddenly smell its foulness

and it was awful. I checked the soles of my shoes, but there was no poo on them. I smelled my hands—that's where the smell was coming from! Somehow I had gotten crap on my hands and hadn't known! I went and washed them and the tools I had touched, then came back to finish setting up my sap collection with a makeshift tap and bucket to funnel the sap into, but there was the smell again—that stench of shit! After much confusion I realized that it was this tree's sap that stunk so horribly. I have never heard of or seen this before or since, but the sap was a dark brown colour (it is usually clear as the clearest water) and stunk unimaginably.

Years later I found that the tree had come down in a storm, and when I looked closely the wood appeared to have been infected with a fungal disease, discolored and dark. Apparently this disease makes sap that is functionally equivalent to those stink bombs sold at novelty shops—perhaps a sustainable alternative?

Being in a place for a while lets one see bigger stories unfold. The one I really want to talk about, though, is succession.

There is another place I used to often visit as a child, a steep ravine with a creek flowing through its center that friends and I would walk through on our way to the ocean. When I was about 12, one of the slopes of this ravine slipped. A landslide swiftly brought all of the sword ferns, alders and fir trees down to the bottom and left the slope barren. Within a year or two, however, the slope was anything but naked; Scotch broom had completely cloaked the steep soil, which seemed to enrage everyone in the neighborhood.

Scotch broom (Cytisus scoparius) is an introduced, European "invasive" shrub. It is extremely resilient, thriving typically in areas that have suffered some kind of cataclysmic event that has left the soil bare, damaged and subject to erosion. Such cataclysmic events are almost without exception created

by human activity (even the ravine mentioned above was itself the result of severe erosion from clear-cut logging in the
19th century). From a biological standpoint, Scotch broom is a
godsend; its ability to stabilize bare earth, increase soil fertility
(broom is a member of the legume family, like beans and peas,
increasing soil fertility by drawing atmospheric nitrogen into
it) and thrive in the worst of conditions, covering and healing
the wounded earth, far surpasses that of any native plant.

Strangely, as with many other successful, introduced
"weeds" (the great Japanese kudzu vine in the United States,
Himalayan blackberry across the northwest, broom's close relative gorse, to name a few), most people are in agreement that
they deeply hate this invasive plant. Environmentalists even
go so far as to organize Scotch broom pulls where people get
together to try and clear a piece of land of this pitiful plant
for good. To quote Jim Pojar and Andy MacKinnon from
their authoritative reference guide to plants of the Northwest:
"Broom has been so successful over much of its range that it
has endangered much of our region's distinctive rain shadow
flora." This is *almost* true. People's hatred for broom (and various other invasive plants) is *almost* based in reality. A statement that comes closer to the truth might be: "Civilization
has been so successful over much of its range that it has endangered much of our region's distinctive rain shadow flora.
Into this desperate situation enters broom." Scotch broom,
like many of its invasive colleagues, is a symptom of destruction, not a cause, in much the same way that poverty-stricken,
drug-riddled, violent ghettos are the symptom of a broken system, not the cause of societal problems. Broom will not sprout
up on the shady floor of an ancient forest and choke out all of
the big old spruce and cedar, leaving a desert in its wake. There
is only one invasive species capable of that: the domesticated
human.

But back to that ravine. As I said, a few years after the land-slide, that slope was completely engulfed in vigorous broom plants. The whole scene would turn a brilliant yellow every spring when they went into bloom. On hot, quiet summer days seedpods would explode open with non-stop crackle-pops. It was only a few months ago, when walking through the old ravine for the first time in years, that I noticed how things had changed.

The broom was gone.

I swear, all that was left in remembrance of its once abso-lute, glorious reign were some grey, brittle old skeletons, half decayed. It hadn't been cut, it had been left alone and lived out its natural life cycle—apparently a fairly brief one of about 10–15 years. The steep bank is now cloaked in a scraggly mix of Himalayan blackberry vines and red alder saplings reaching well above the tangled chaos at their feet. In 20 years those alders will be tall and leafy enough that the blackberries will have withered away in their dense shade. The alders will begin shading even one another out, they will grow so thick. Fifty years from then the alders left standing will have gotten old, near the end of their life cycle, dying in their own time, falling and building the soil with their bodies. Climax species such as cedar and hemlock will begin taking their place; the landscape will be getting mature.

It's all just a phase, it's all temporary, constantly moving in a big story of living and dying and nourishing the ground for what's next. The weedy chaos that we see sprouting in the wake of ecological trauma is only one brief chapter in an end-less story, fulfilling a vital need. Land that has been covered in the barbed-wire protection of brambles tells us "Go away, I need space, I'm healing. Oh, and have some of this delicious fruit, too."

It is tempting to see succession as a linear pattern; this is the lens through which civilization frames existence, after all. In reality it is more cyclical or even chaotic. Once a land base gets to its climax ecology, it doesn't stay there. Fire swiftly takes some mature forests back down to the ground as part of their natural cycle. We know that some trees in fact need such devastating fire to sweep through in order for their seed to even germinate. Of course a climax phase of succession can sometimes be measured in centuries or longer, where the weedy, early phases might be measured in decades or years, but the fact remains that succession is an ongoing process. Nothing living remains static. Throughout this cyclical movement life works towards building more soil, biological diversity, uniqueness and intelligence.

What I am really interested in is how this pattern of ecological succession applies to human societies, and what it might reveal about where we are headed. We are living creatures, after all, so shouldn't some principles of ecological healing, renewal and change apply to us?

If an area of land that has been devastated by human activity or natural disaster is simply left alone, it will heal. But to really get to the point, this is the big question: What about humans? If we take away the governing bodies, the structures that propel us to destroy our land base and each other; if the forces that domesticate us were to cease and we were allowed to go feral, like a hillside engulfed in blackberry vines, would we naturally find balance and heal, like all other living things?

At this point I think the answer is an obvious no. The great difference between us and all other living things is, once again, our conditioning. The fact that humans are their own enemy in the game of domestication (the source of such conditioning) complicates everything.

Remove all the oppressive forces, leave modern humans alone to go feral, and what do you think will happen? Almost without question they will simply create new oppressive structures, enact the same patterns of abuse as came before. We have to acknowledge the fact that in this culture, broadly speaking, everyone's mind has been infected with poison, whatever shape it may have come in. We also have to acknowledge that most people associate happiness with business as usual: the ability to jump in one's car, grab a six-pack at the liquor store, head over to the grocery store and buy anything, go home, turn the heat up, put on some music and have an hour-long hot shower. If you suddenly take away these luxuries, most people are going to do anything they can to get them back. But step out of civilization's consciousness (also known as denial), and it becomes apparent that all of the above luxuries are the products of a death machine, and that enjoying them typically means participating in and actually signing over your freedom to this machine.

If humans had clean minds, like grasses and thistles, we would return to a state of balance when the forces of domestication ceased. As it is, if civilization were to come down tomorrow, everyone would begin attempting to rebuild it the next day. The mentality that created it in the first place would still exist. The forces of domestication have been internalized. This is why revolutions are called revolutions: the literal meaning is to go around in circles. Perhaps the best ecological analogy for us would be a piece of land left to go feral after an oil spill. That oil spill is going to slow down healing, succession and a return to balance, much like the toxic, civilized mind will. Still, bioremediation techniques can rapidly speed the detoxification of contaminated soil, allowing poisoned land to heal and regrow. We might think of domesticated humans in the same way; there is some initial decontamination work to be done before we can find balance. If we want to truly step out of the cycle of domestication and destruction, we are going to have to become mature, aware, I might even say enlightened creatures. Like salmon.

I went into a Walmart today, and it sent shivers down my spine. There were giant TV screens showing advertisements, no windows, the smell of plastic and perfume, but what really stood out was that there were a *lot* of people in there. They appeared glad enough to be there, though not ecstatic by any means. Standing in line, shopping carts stuffed to the brim with cheap electronics, makeup, buckets of mayonnaise and the like. I'm not trying to pick on Walmart or the people that shop there, I completely understand the reasons many do, but I am reminded every time I enter such an environment that the mass of humanity is still very much entrenched in the mythology of civilization. When I say that we are going to have to become mature, aware, enlightened creatures, I am fully aware how far humanity as a whole is from that. Perhaps the situation parts of the developed world are beginning to find themselves in, where the standard of living is shrinking as empire contracts, will set the stage for this kind of shift. (I am reminded of the old Buddhist proverb: "To attain enlightenment, haul water and chop wood. When you have finished, haul more water.")

What is clear is the necessity of change; humans must, like deer and salmon, welcome and join the weedy chaos that will lead to healing. To actually envision humans integrated into the cycle of succession is a beautiful thing. At first it will likely look ragged, chaotic and confusing, then eventually move towards something more balanced, preparing the ground for what is to come next. Like the invasive weeds I mentioned above, given the right conditions, sanity may be contagious, it may spread and flourish. And as with the invasive weeds above, the domesticated mind will always see this as an assault on order. Luckily, at least some of us know that that order itself is insane.

As forests rise and fall, consumed by fire, so do civilizations. All civilizations have a life cycle, collapse is inevitable. Whether humans simply build a new empire in the wake of collapse is up in the air.

Maybe it's time to evolve.

CHAPTER 11

Killing The Most Beautiful Thing

Who could love a creature more
than the one that kills it,
takes its flesh into their body,
depends on it for survival
and sees the world through its eyes?

I RECENTLY KILLED A DEER. It's not the first time I have done this, and likely won't be the last. I could tell the story like this: The frozen stillness of the woods, full moon reflected on snow all night and at first light the roar of the nearby highway drowned out by adrenaline as he and I stare into each others eyes. For a moment. I shoot, he dies.

After he has been laying down for a couple of minutes I get close enough to touch him—a massive beautiful creature. He still feels so alive, muscles warm and loose. I kneel down and hug him—there aren't many other opportunities for hugging a buck like this—just for being so close to a creature so beautiful and powerful. Eventually, I drag him in the snow away from the deer trail, to gut him. But first I wait a while and just look at him in complete awe, before I cut open and start dismantling his perfect body.

Something about this relationship is particularly fascinating to me. I honestly feel like that deer, and every deer I have ever killed, is the most beautiful creature I've ever seen. And

I killed it. And somehow this makes complete sense to me, though somehow it sounds like it shouldn't at all.

Knowing who I have killed in order to eat, to maintain my own life, I carry the burden of taking something extremely beautiful out of this world. A beauty that I can never replace. I owe that deer. I know this, because I killed him. How I can repay what I owe to that deer and the world I took it from I might never know. But I will try.

And because I killed him, because I saw him in grace and power, then in pain and confusion expiring that last breath, it's just between us, and something bigger too, but I know what I took because I did it. The loss and sadness are mine to carry. There is something refreshingly clean about this.

The food we buy and feel a clean conscience eating, while the hunter's hands are stained with blood — that is more confusing. It's clear to see that a human killing a wild animal is somewhat sad, because humans don't know how to live well on this Earth.

What it needs are more amazing wild creatures and fewer humans, not the opposite. What is unclear is how sad consuming any plant or animal as food is, if we are disconnected from how it came to us.

Food from the store, as a rule, kills much more beauty, destroys unimaginably more life, than a hunt like the one I described above. It is invisible killing, to the consumer at least, because it is culturally accepted. Rivers drained to irrigate crops (yes, even organic ones), habitat destruction and displacement of wildlife, the constant eradication of undesirable plant and animal species. Fossil fuels. Migrant labor. To actually wrap one's head around how much suffering and loss went into their "guilt-free" bowl of organic whole grains with tofu, tamari and flax oil is probably not possible. There is no guilt-free food option for us (except for maybe bankers, politicians and the like, if you're into that) and there shouldn't be. I don't walk around feeling awful all the time because I need to kill to live (or have someone else do it for me), I love acknowledging that bittersweet reality and how complex it is. It is part of being alive — the essence of being alive.

We all owe a lot. And I owe that deer.

II

endangered skills

CHAPTER 12

Learning How to Live

IT IS OFTEN SAID that people will stay in an abusive relationship so long as they depend, or think they depend, on
their abuser. On one level this could be a woman staying with
a partner that beats, degrades and controls her, out of fear that
she would not be able to survive on her own without his material support. On another level, it is how our culture functions
as a whole. People work dead-end jobs and live dead-end lives
in a dead-end society because they know no other way. We
depend on those jobs and that society for our food, clothing,
shelter and medical needs.

There can be no fundamental change in this culture, or in
any abusive relationship based on domination and control,
until we realize we can support ourselves without it and learn
how. This is no small task. Fortunately for us, though, this
journey is filled with color, life, sensuality and connection. As
much as it is a strategic necessity, this task can be looked at as
a fascinating, magical path of coming to know the breathing,
pulsing, sacred living world.

Learning how to live, how to provide the fundamentals of
human existence for ourselves, is at the very heart of rewilding. Only in the context of real-life interaction can we come

89

90 UNLEARN, REWILDREWILD

to know the non-human world, build relationships with it and ensure that those relationships are healthy. Only with the skills of survival can we approach freedom.

What comes next is a collection of endangered skills, skills that have been fast disappearing along with traditional societies. The topics I have chosen to include here run a broad spectrum, from scavenging roadkill to natural contraception. Instead of following the usual formula survival guides use (chapters on fire, plant food, animal food, shelter, stone tools), I have decided to offer skills that have been particularly relevant during my own time living on the land, and that are unique, shrouded in obscurity or truly endangered. Though some of these skills will appeal to hobbyists, they were learned and are being shared within the context of everyday life. A radically different type of everyday life than the accepted norm: a down-and-dirty, sane and sustainable everyday life. They are offered as tools to help us live sustainably and connect, intimately, to the wildness within and without.

CHAPTER 13

Honoring the Bodies of Animals—
By Eating Them

L EARNING HOW TO fully utilize the bodies of animals as food from books and conventional hunters can be a disempowering process; countless myths abound surrounding how to handle meat and what conditions will "spoil" it. I received a lot of fear-filled, paranoid and straight-up false information when first trying to figure out how to process animals. Thankfully a few teachers who wound up in my life enabled me to move beyond the untested myths that are so prevalent and limiting in this area. Here I have made an attempt to counter all of the conventional information out there with something a little more empowering, traditional and based in reality, as opposed to our bland, modern cultural norms.

According to Conventional Wisdom

Here are some classic examples of advice often given by butchers and conventional hunters (I would call myself an un-conventional hunter) that can be misleading.

- After killing a deer one must *immediately* gut the creature and get the carcass down to a "safe" temperature of three degrees Celsius or lower. Any intestinal contents that come into contact with meat will completely spoil it.

- Maggots will spoil any meat they come into contact with.
- Hair that contacts the meat will spoil it.
- Puncturing the scent glands will assuredly cause spoilage.
- If a creature has stiffened (rigor mortis has set in), it has spoiled.
- Basically, once the creature has been killed, it is a race against time to remove the guts and get the carcass cooled as fast as possible. Failure to do so will result in bacteria mysteriously spoiling all of the meat.

I was even told by one hunter, "Deer fat is tallow, what they make soap out of—if you don't cut all of that tallow off your meat it's gonna taste soapy." I am sure now that he had never eaten deer tallow or soap—they taste absolutely nothing alike—not to mention that eating any quantity of lean meat without fat has a toxic effect on the body (more on this later). Deer tallow is a healthy and delicious edible fat. Even if it isn't your thing, it won't be because of the resemblance to soap.

The ridiculously bad advice you might receive from hunters and butchers is limited only by their imagination. If all of what they say is true, we would pretty much never be able to safely salvage the bodies of dead animals. For most of human history, however, humans did not have access to freezers, walk-in coolers, latex gloves or any of the other necessities of modern, sterile animal processing.

Pygmy hunter-gatherers in present-day Africa, for instance, would kill an elephant, which the family or clan then camped around until they had finished eating and drying it. This is at temperatures of probably over 30 degrees Celsius, often for a week or more, as they worked through the massive creature. Caribou-hunting Inuit cached whole dead caribou, which had only been gutted, out on the open tundra in improvised rock coverings for a year or more.

Danish explorer Knud Rasmussen wrote of his time with the Netsilik Inuit:

> Right alongside the spot where we pitched our camp we found an old cache of caribou meat — two years old I was told. We cleared the stones away and fed the dogs, for it is law in this country that as soon as a cache is more than a winter and a summer old, it falls to the one who has use for it. The meat was green with age, and when we made a cut in it, it was like the bursting of a boil, so full of great white maggots was it. To my horror my companions scooped out handfuls of the crawling things and ate them with evident relish. I criticized their taste, but they laughed at me and said, not illogically: *"You yourself like caribou meat, and what are these maggots but live caribou meat? They taste just the same as the meat and are refreshing to the mouth."*

Clearly different people have different ideas and methods for handling meat. An indigenous approach is more concerned with honoring the body of the creature by taking the most nourishment possible from it, where the modern attitude is to use only some of the creature's body if it is convenient, sterile and socially acceptable.

Roadkill

Roadkilled animals are an excellent place to start learning how to make the best use of creatures' bodies and also to challenge conventional wisdom. It is illegal to salvage roadkill in many places, so learn your local laws and act appropriately. Whether that means following them is up to you.

Getting the guts out as soon as possible *is* a good thing to do — digestive juices and anaerobic conditions are pretty much the main forces that degrade meat. I want to emphasize,

though, that there are no rules. Often a deer that has been
laying in the ditch for two days in the fall will have very little
or no meat tainted by gastric juices. Also, the front legs of a
deer are far enough away from the digestive organs that they
are sometimes not contaminated even when everything else is.
Even the worst roadkills often have something salvageable —
bits of meat, hide, hooves, head — for one with the desire and
ambition.

Here are some ways to tell how long a roadkilled animal
has been dead for:

- Does the hair pull out easily when you tug on it? If not, it's
  somewhat fresh. If so, it may be a sign that the creature has
  been there for a while, but not a definite sign of spoilage by
  any means.
- Are the eyes clouded over? If not, it's pretty fresh.
- Are the creature's arms and legs stiff? Rigor mortis sets in
  anywhere from ten minutes to several hours after death,
  but only lasts less than a day. This means that if the joints
  are stiff, a roadkill is relatively fresh (less than a day old).

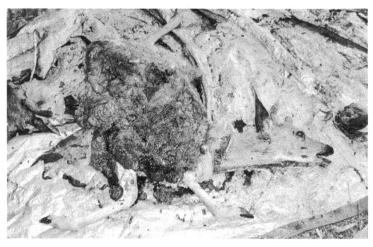

A worst case scenario roadkilled deer. Most roadkill scavengers would
simply pass up a carcass that had been smashed this severely.

- Are full-sized maggots crawling around on it? They usually take a day at least to go from little maggot eggs to full-sized crawly maggots. In hot summer weather, however, this maturation can happen in hours.
- On a hot summer day, a roadkill will degrade fairly quickly, the heat from its digestive system and eventually the digestive juices themselves permeating the meat with a strong, acquired flavor. In the winter, however, creatures can stay longer on the side of the road (or dead in the forest) without the flavor or texture of the meat being affected.
- As a rule, smaller creatures keep better on the roadside, their smaller digestive systems produce less heat and don't permeate meat with gastric flavors as quickly. Rabbits will last longer with their guts intact than, say, elk.

One recommended method for saving badly smashed roadkills is to completely gut the creature, wipe away any spilled stomach and intestinal contents, then cut off the surface of any areas that have been contaminated by them. Often just the

An amazing save! A talented scavenger was able to salvage this meat from that poor mangled deer and, after marinating, have some delicious meals.

surface of the meat takes on the strong taste and odor, unless it has been long enough for the gastric juices to really permeate the meat. Even then, the meat can be marinated or spiced up and is still totally safe to eat. Many roadkilled creatures are just hit in the head, and are actually tidier to gut and butcher than if they had been shot in their vitals (heart or lungs).

What Actually Causes "Spoilage"?

Only a few main factors cause meat to degrade rapidly or make it unsafe to eat.

Digestive juices. Whether from the dead creature itself or from maggots secreting their own digestive juices onto the meat to break it down (they don't have an internal digestive system the way we do), these fluids cause meat to develop a "hard-to-stomach" taste and lose its structural integrity pretty quickly. They don't make it poisonous, though. Many friends have eaten quantities of deer meat which had been intensely marinated in gastric juices — *raw* — with no ill effect. You might have to build up your stamina to have the same results. Seasoning and cooking such meat can make it delicious and completely safe. That said, digestive juices do "spoil" meat, in the sense of causing it to break down, turn blue and stink.

Anaerobic Conditions. Putting raw meat into plastic bags, buckets or other airtight containers creates an anaerobic environment in which many bacteria flourish that can turn the meat toxic to humans as well as degrading it rapidly the way gastric juices do. Among these bacteria are those that cause botulism. Always try to keep raw meat, organs, etc. stored in an open, ventilated environment, unless they are quite cool and they won't be stored for long.

Ground meat can also foster anaerobic bacteria because of the spaces created in its reconstituted form, making it a risky food to leave sitting around for any amount of time before eating.

Moisture. If meat is left out exposed to rain, it will degrade much faster. Unless marinating, keep it dry!

Aging

Aging meat usually means hanging it somewhere shady, dry, protected from flies and with air circulating around it (not in a plastic bag!). In this state bacteria and enzymes in the meat transform or predigest it, resulting in more tender, flavorful, enzymatically active and easily digested meat. The aging process can take anywhere from two days to several weeks, which flies in the face of the common North American assumption that meat must be kept in a refrigerator, and only for a few days, before it spoils. I am guessing the reason we all grew up thinking meat had to be refrigerated or it would go bad and make us sick was because it is usually in plastic packages or ground, both situations that foster the growth of pathogenic bacteria. To be aged, meat should be well ventilated and not ground.

For more information refer to the next chapter, "Feral Food Preservation."

Parasites and Diseases

What about parasites and diseases we can get from handling and eating dead creatures? I have mentioned eating raw meat quite a bit because cooking red meat at high temperatures (grilling, frying) is known to make it slightly carcinogenic— something to take into account if you're eating significant amounts of it.

My solution is to eat most of the meat I consume raw—usually dried. Parasites are a valid concern, especially if you are also eating other foods that will put you at greater risk of a pathogenic infestation (processed foods, concentrated sugars, grains, etc.).

According to the USDA, freezing any fish or meat for 14 days completely eliminates parasites and parasite eggs. Other ways of eliminating parasites are acid or saline marinades, using vinegar or lemon juice (diluted in water) for the acid or salt dissolved in water for the saline. I don't know specifically how strong is strong enough. You could try pouring your marinade on an open cut and see how much it hurts. Little parasite eggs are pretty sensitive to slight changes in acidity/alkalinity as well as to salt; it doesn't take much.

I will admit that I am fairly relaxed about eating the meat from healthy herbivores either rare or raw, but when it comes to omnivores, one need be much more careful.

Omnivores

Everything I have said so far about eating raw meat applies to *herbivores* only! *Omnivores* are a whole other story, and carry many parasites that are far more serious.

Common omnivorous mammals you might meet include bears, raccoons, the whole weasel family, cats, dogs, rats, seals—the list is long. All omnivore meat can contain trichinosis, a condition caused by parasites in the flesh of raw or undercooked omnivores (pork is the most famous culprit). It can enter the central nervous system and cause serious neurological damage and death. It is one of the scariest of all potential diseases or parasites commonly associated with meat. Sure ways of avoiding or eliminating it include thoroughly cooking (cat is better stewed than raw anyways) and freezing the meat for at least 14 days. Other heavy hitters include hantavirus, rabies and chronic wasting disease. Hantavirus and rabies are both destroyed by cooking; the main risk is during processing. Chronic wasting disease is fairly geographically isolated; if you live where it is prevalent (the Midwestern prairies of North America are the area of most concern), educate yourself. Omnivore meat is not guaranteed to make you sick if you eat it undercooked or raw, but the general rule is to treat it as though it would. Cook the meat thoroughly, don't handle it if you have open wounds, and educate yourself on the real and perceived risks. Contact local authorities and organizations related to wildlife, visit government websites and talk to knowledgeable hunters. Cross reference the information you get from various sources to find common threads of truth.

The Whole Body

Many hunters tell stories about killing a deer, gutting it, deboning the meat and packing it out of the bush in a backpack, leaving the rest of the body behind. Morally I don't think there is anything wrong with leaving so much food in the forest for the bears and raccoons, but as far as getting the most nourishment from the animal's body and honoring it, much more can be done. Organs such as the liver, kidneys, heart, pancreas and testicles are nutrient-dense superfoods, much more so than muscle meat. Any fat on a healthy creature's body is usually delicious and nutritious, a gift to be treasured as opposed to something unhealthy to get rid of.

- The adrenal glands have the highest vitamin C content of any plant or animal tissue known. They can be found in a ball of fat above or beneath the kidneys.
- Eyes are a concentrated source of zinc which, coincidentally, they require to function well.
- Bones are filled with marrow—basically a mineral rich fat. If you have large enough quantities (I have, once) it can be

rendered the same way as chunks of body fat are. We usually just eat it raw.

- Bones can also be simmered into mineral rich-broths (see below), as well as fashioned into tools.
- Hooves and soft, velvet antlers can also can be simmered into a gelatin or mineral-rich broth that is a delicious and strong medicine.
- Brains can be removed from the head and used to tan hides or eaten like scrambled eggs (delicious!).
- The pancreas, smaller but quite similar in appearance to the liver, is the most concentrated source of vitamin K-2, a factor that has been used to treat and prevent tooth decay and other forms of physical degeneration. It is covered in a chewy membrane that you can peel off before preparing and eating the tender organ beneath.
- Testicles are a delicious libido-enhancing food. They taste very much like hot dogs.
- Hides can be brain-tanned, bark-tanned, made into rawhide, glue, cord, etc. If you aren't inspired to do anything with them then freeze, salt or dry them and find a friend who is.

Bone Broth

Bone broths are a highly nutritious, medicinal base for many contemporary gourmet soups and sauces, and have traditionally been a vital source of easily assimilated minerals, fats and unique proteins like cartilage and tendons. Using bones and hooves to make broth can greatly stretch the amount of food and food value one gets from a creature's body. For larger mammals, the marrow bones are best for broth. These are the long marrow-filled shafts that make up the front and hind legs. Break or use a hacksaw to open these bones, place in a pot with water and a teaspoon of vinegar to help draw out minerals. Rainwater, being essentially distilled, will draw out minerals quite actively without added vinegar. Simmer gently for 24–72 hours for large bones (a wood stove or solar oven are most practical for this), 3–6 hrs for bird carcasses or fish spines. This provides good bone-building medicine for a culture whose teeth are chronically crumbling.

The list of potential uses is actually endless. Suffice it to say that the whole body is a gift if we know how to use it.

So, don't be afraid. It's actually a really beautiful thing to honor the body of an animal by using it.

CHAPTER 14

Feral Food Preservation: Unconventional and Traditional Methods of Putting Things By

P RESERVING FOOD is often as much of an art and skill as procuring it. In many instances it eclipses harvesting in the amount of time and care it takes. The ability to simply bag food and throw it in the freezer has replaced what not long ago were countless methods for preserving specific foods, methods that often transformed and enhanced their taste, texture and nutritional value.

At first, storing food without electricity, disconnected from an industrial support system, may seem like an insurmountable problem. Without a fridge or freezer, we've been told, meat will spoil almost instantaneously. How do we dry food without a dehydrator? Especially in the middle of winter? How can we keep perishable foods without canning them? I attempt to answer these and more questions here.

Prior to the Industrial Revolution, foods were most often preserved using three major, widespread techniques: drying, cool storage/cellaring and fermentation. As well, heavily salting, smoking, storing in oil, vinegar, alcohol, ashes and other methods have all been employed to greater or lesser extents among different peoples.

Traditional preservation methods are fun, lend themselves to experimentation and regional variation and are sustainable and free. They seem to be the culinary antithesis of modern, mass-produced, predictable, industrial foodstuffs. Because they are unpredictable and alive, using some of these methods to process and preserve our food can bring us more in touch with the magic of being a creature and eating.

I have separated plant and animal foods into two categories, the preparation and concerns around them being so distinct.

Plant Foods

Drying

Drying food may appear to be so simple it's not worth mentioning. I still remember, though, feeling like a dehydrator was an incredibly necessary and irreplaceable tool. It isn't. Anything you can dry in a dehydrator can be dried by the sun and air, or in a dry cabin, home or shed with a heat source in it. The same conditions that will dry your wet clothes will dry fresh (wet) food. And the same principles for hanging clothes to dry in the sun or by the stove apply—in order for moisture to escape, the clothes or food need to have air flow around them. If they are too close to the stove they will get burned, if it takes too long they'll get moldy. Bring them in at night or cover them to protect them from dew. Drying food leaves enzymes and vitamins intact, unless left to dry for too long, and if sun-dried even fortifies certain foods (mushrooms in particular) with vitamin D and deactivates anti-nutrients like oxalic acid which is contained in some leafy greens and interferes with mineral metabolism.

Tree Fruit

Apples. Core or pit and slice. If you don't mind chewing a bit more, just slice them into rounds and the seeds will likely fall out after they dry. Eating a few is supposed to be good—they contain B-17, an anti-carcinogenic vitamin, but are toxic in quantity. Put the slices on screens or racks or thread them onto a string. If you core your apples use that hole for stringing. Apples are very forgiving, they can dry slowly on screens or strings in an attic over a week.

Another method of drying apples, perhaps not as efficient but fun and tasty, is to bake them until soft (prick some holes in the skin for this), smush them into cakes and then dry. This is a forgotten traditional dessert of the British Isles, well suited to those who prefer their apples cooked.

Pears. Slice into halves, quarters or thinner and lay on racks or screens as per apples. A traditional Slovak method of preserving pears involves drying them whole. Harvest small varieties in the fall, after they have dropped off the tree and turned golden brown—not rotten, just fully ripe. Apparently there is a word for this state in Slovak. They are then dried whole on screens above a wood stove. The result is a chewy, sweet treat akin to dried dates or figs. At first the pears will get dark and very soft, then start wrinkling and drying. Depending on the pears and temperature (preferably quite warm), this can take a week or more. Have patience.

Cherries, apricots, plums and other softer fruits. Remove the pits, halve and dry in the sun. The moister, softer and sweeter the fruit, the faster mold will flourish, so the quicker they need to be dried.

Berries. Berries in the *rubus* clan and their kin (black raspberry, thimbleberry, blackberry) can be dried whole in the sun or any other very warm environment or mashed and formed into cakes, so that moisture can more easily escape, and dried on screens or racks. They need to dry in a few days or mold will form. The above applies to other thin-skinned berries like strawberry and salal.

Berries in the *vaccinium* clan like blueberries, red huckleberries, bilberries and saskatoons lend themselves to being dried whole. They can be dried slowly, over weeks even, in a well ventilated dry space. I've dried wild blueberries over several weeks in an unheated, well-ventilated cabin. No mold formed and they were even slightly fermented, increasing their nutrient content. Rosehips and other small, firm fruit can be treated in the same way.

Vegetables

Vegetables often don't lend themselves to drying as readily as fruits. Fermentation is a more appropriate method for preserving many (cabbage, kale and other hardy greens), while roots are often cellared or stored whole in their natural state. There are times it does make sense though.

Shoots and leaves. Dry on racks or screens until they are crispy or will break when bent. Drying in the shade versus full sun, as well as at moderate temperatures, helps preserve nutrients, volatile oils and other medicinal constituents in plants. A shady, breezy location is ideal; a well-ventilated shed or room works well.

Roots. Slice thin, or quarter into carrot-sticks and dry on racks or screens. To dry roots even faster, grate them to expose more moisture to evaporation.

Fermentation

Traditional cultures have used fermentation as a method of storing vegetables for millennia. It actually *increases* vitamin and enzyme content, and if done properly, many fermented foods will keep for six months to a year. The basic principle behind fermenting vegetables is to keep them submerged under brine, which is either their own juice or salted water. Under the anaerobic protection of this brine, lactic-acid-forming bacteria go to work eating and excreting, changing the acidity of the fermentation and making it more storable, as well as enhancing the enzyme and vitamin content.

Sauerkraut is probably the most well-known vegetable ferment. It is made by slicing or grating cabbage, lightly salting it to get the juices flowing, and pounding the shredded, salted cabbage bit by bit into a container until it is submerged under its own juices, weighed down and allowed to ferment under the anaerobic protection of a salty brine. Using the principle that vegetables submerged in a salty brine (often their own juices) will be colonized by beneficial bacteria which enhance their flavor, nutrition and storability leads to endless possibilities.

Roots can be grated, lightly salted to extract juices and mushed into a jar, then submerged to ferment. Many leafy vegetables can be chopped or grated and processed in the same manner. Fermentation occurs more rapidly at higher temperatures: the bacteria we are encouraging thrive at a temperature of 18–25 degrees Celsius. Anything much higher and they will not thrive, anything lower and they will simply take longer to culture your food.

Fermenting vegetables can be stored at room temperature for a week or more, to activate fermentation, then moved to a cooler, cellar-like temperature to "ripen" or mature over months. Here are a couple of ways to preserve a wild root vegetable, burdock, that illustrate the basic technique that can be applied to so many other veggies.

Pickled Burdock

Version 1: sliced. Clean dirt off burdock roots (preferably tender, mid-sized roots), slice into carrot-stick-sized strips (quarters or eighths). Pack into a sterilized jar with warm, salted water (two to three tablespoons salt to one quart water, leaning towards more in warmer months when lactic-acid-forming bacteria will have more competition and less in cooler months) cover with a lid or cloth and let sit at room temperature for one week. After one week, they can be moved to a cooler space to ripen further.

Version 2: grated. Again, take clean, tender burdock roots, but this time grate them into a bowl. Add salt to this grated burdock (one-half to one tablespoon salt for one quart of grated vegetable, leaning again towards more in warm summer months). Allowing it to sit salted for a few minutes will get its juices flowing. Bit by bit, mush this salted burdock into a sterilized jar. Pack it in forcefully, one handful at a time, making sure it gets stuffed in tightly and the vegetables are submerged in juice. Cover with a lid or cloth. Again allow to sit at room temperature for one week. This recipe will mature faster than version 1 as grating allows fermentation to act more quickly.

The following recipe does not require any salt, making it unique and useful if you don't have access to that precious resource. It's called Gundru, and is the national food of Nepal. The leaves of any hardy green (kale, collard, mustard, chard, beet) can be used—it is essentially pickled greens.

Gundru

If you are using kale (that's what I usually have around), you'll probably notice the light powder that coats the leaves. This is yeast, just like the light covering of yeast on grapes. It will help activate the fermentation, so don't wash it off. The next step is optional: let the kale wilt in the sun. I don't fully understand what the purpose of this step is; it could be partially ceremonial (welcoming sun medicine into the greens?), it could begin breaking down cell walls to make the next steps easier. Make sure to just let the kale wilt, not dry out, you need those juices. You could skip this step; I have and it still worked.

Now you need to crush and smush the kale to really get the juices flowing. A rolling pin (or wine bottle or jar) on a board works for this—use some force. Try not to lose the juices. When the kale has been crushed, pack it into a jar as tightly as possible. Do this bit by bit. Crush some kale, stuff it into the jar and tamp it in really well with a bottle, piece of wood, whatever will fit in there. Again, use some force—you might be surprised how much kale can fit into a small jar. After a while, dark green juice should cover the kale when you push down with your tool. By the time your jar is almost full you won't be able to push down without juices overflowing. Don't let them out! When you are at this point, add enough smushed greens so that when you put a lid on, the juices come right to the top.

Now put your gundru someplace warm and let it sit for one to three weeks. Put something under it like a plate as it has a tendency to bubble and ooze out juices as it ferments. When you eventually can't wait any longer, or remember you forgot about it, open it up. It should smell and taste sharp and tangy, really good. If it's not tangy at all, either the wrong bacteria took over (don't eat it) or it is too young. It can be eaten fresh or dried in the sun. When it gets crispy-dry it tastes like ketchup-flavored potato chips (in the very best way possible). Dried, it can be used as an enzyme-rich green condiment or snack. It is really good fresh, though. It also stores for quite long if you don't open it. We've had gundru stored for over a year, through a hot summer and frozen winter—it was totally delicious (and didn't make us sick). I don't open a jar of gundru and then plan to store it for another couple of months, it needs to be eaten or dried within a few weeks or so of opening, though refrigeration might change that.

Fermenting Fruit

A traditional Finnish method of storing wild blueberries involves mashing them into a jam, and stuffing this blueberry mash without any further ado into sterilized jars for storage. The lids used are smeared with a bit of honey, which acts either to enhance the seal around the rim of the jar or as an antimicrobial barrier between the jar and the outside world.

Mashed wild blueberries stored in this way will keep for up to a year in a cool place. Presumably the inherent acidity of the fruit and the activity of beneficial bacteria are the main agents of preservation. Cultivated blueberries are not as acidic as wild species and may not be suitable. Other similar, high-acid berries, like evergreen huckleberry and cranberry, may work well.

Water Storage

Wild crabapples can be stored for many months simply by submerging them in water. Pick them when still firm and they will become soft, delicious and slightly fermented after being kept under water someplace cool for a month or so. If a film of mold forms on the surface of the water, simply skim it off—it's harmless. Some apple cultivars may have been stored in water traditionally as well; a friend shared with me a story about a wheelbarrow of storage apples she never got around to storing, the wheelbarrow was forgotten and left out in the rain for months. When she finally got around to dealing with it, she decided to taste one of the drowned apples. To her surprise it was totally fine. She kept those apples until spring under water. Perhaps that is where bobbing for apples comes from?

Cranberries and other high-acid, firm-skinned fruits also have traditionally been stored in water.

Cool Storage

Many roots, along with some fruits and vegetables, will keep through the winter simply if they are kept dry and cool (but not frozen).

Crabapples preserved in water.

Apples, potatoes, beets and most other roots can simply be stored in boxes, someplace where they won't get either too warm or freeze. Freezing and thawing breaks down the cell walls, making things mushy (and eventually rotten). A box in a cool corner, covered in some blankets or what-have-you for insulation is usually sufficient. An actual cellar is great if you have access to one — any place that is cool but doesn't freeze will suffice.

Start with unbruised fruit or vegetables and sort through the boxes every few weeks, culling any rotten ones (one bad apple can spoil the whole bunch). Some roots, like burdock and carrots, are better stored in sand. This is done by layering slightly damp sand with roots in a container, or on the ground somewhere dry (a cellar, an overhang). This keeps them from drying or shriveling and protects them from freezing. A friend has kept beets in good condition for two years this way, stored in boxes of layered, slightly damp sand, under the overhang of his roof (through the mild winters of the Pacific Northwest, keep in mind).

Another friend stores her fall-harvested cranberries through the winter simply by putting the unbruised fruits into a wooden box and keeping them under her house where it never freezes but always stays cool (in the Canadian sub-arctic!).

Animal Foods

Drying

The same principles outlined for drying plant foods apply here. If you can dry your clothes you can dry meat.

Jerky can be made by thinly slicing meat from mammals or fish a quarter-inch thick, give or take, and hanging it on strings in the sun or in a heated structure. Traditionally, under certain circumstances, smoke has been used as part of this process to keep flies at bay and to add creosote, a preservative. Creosote is carcinogenic, so I do not usually smoke meat at all if there is an alternative. When drying meat outdoors under the sun, one can avoid flies laying maggots by choosing a windy site and a sunny location and slicing the meat thinly. The maggots, not the flies, are the real problem; they will eat the meat and secrete digestive juices on it that will make it taste kind of gross, though still edible. Once the meat forms a hard crust

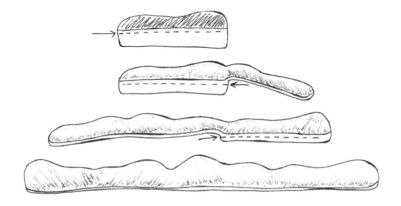

The butterfly cut.

on the outside, flies will not be able to lay maggot eggs on it. Wasps can be an issue as
well. Again, if you dry it fast they won't
have much of a chance to gorge. If
you have a mosquito net, that will
work wonderfully as protection.
By making a butterfly cut—
one continuous cut rather than
multiple slices—you can create
one large strip of meat for hanging and drying, rather than multiple

A tripod with meat hanging
to dry outdoors.

small strips. This reduces the amount of space needed and the
work in flipping and removing the jerky.

Drying meat indoors with the help of a wood stove (or
however your structure is heated) works great. Simply set up
some strings above, but well away from, your heat source and
hang the meat on them. Once one side of the meat has dried,
open up or flip the pieces so the inside gets some air flow.

Meat is done drying when crispy. It will be brittle and
crack somewhat when bent in the hands.

Some indigenous people have traditionally dried meat in
well-ventilated stone huts situated in very windy locations.
The meat dries by wind alone, illustrating how essential air
flow is. The following is a list of other body parts that dry well.

- Liver: This is quite tasty dried, somewhat sweet. Slice and
  hang as per muscle meat.
- Lung: Kind of fluffy like popcorn when dried. Slice and
  hang it.
- Eyeballs: If you have a bunch of fish (or other) heads, get
  those eyeballs out, put them on a screen and dry. They take
  a few days and are a crunchy, salty tasting, highly nutritious snack and a dense source of precious vitamins and
  minerals.

- Blood: Place blood in a shallow dish—glass or ceramic are ideal—and let it sit somewhere the moisture can evaporate. Flies and wasps do not seem to care for blood, so don't worry about them. When dry, break it out of the dish, crumble it up and use it as a supplement or energy food. Very powerful stuff.
- Visceral fat: Some ruminant mammals (deer, elk, cow, sheep, moose) have considerable stores of fat surrounding their organs or viscera. This fat can be rendered for storage, or simply hung to dry if one would prefer to eat it raw. It should be dried only until all moisture is gone and not under intense heat or it will render (drip liquid oil). Dried raw visceral fat is wonderful to eat with dried meat—an incredibly nutritious delicacy. Only bother doing this with the fat of herbivores. The fats of omnivores and carnivores (including fish, birds and marine mammals) will simply liquefy or render during drying. Hanging chunks will end up dripping grease beneath them and will remain oily pieces of slick fat. The fat of herbivorous mammals begins in a more solid state and remains that way.

Experiment with other organs and body parts.

Smoking

Having said above that smoking is not the healthiest choice for preserving meat, I understand that it does taste quite good and the creosote acts as a powerful preservative. Also, in some circumstances smoke is necessary to keep flies and wasps at bay. There are two main ways of smoking meat: hot smoking and cold smoking. Hot smoking is more simple and traditional: meat is slowly dried by the gentle warmth of a smoky fire in an enclosed space (the smokehouse). The creosote that collects on its surface enhances flavor and shelf life. Cold smoking is more complex, requiring smoke to be channeled from a fire into a separate chamber where it infuses into the meat without drying it. This is more for flavor than preservation, as the undried meat will still be subject to spoilage. I'll only describe hot smoking here, with the warning that I personally do not smoke any significant amount of my own everyday food for health reasons.

Any ramshackle shed can be used as a smokehouse, with adequate ventilation at the top that allows smoke to escape. You don't want to cook the meat or fish here, just slowly dry it. Cooking will reduce storability. In your smokehouse, build a fire using hardwood (alder, maple, oak, etc.) until you have a good bed of coals, then smother it with green, fresh or wet hardwood, so that it produces more smoke and less fire. The coals should be strong enough that they will stay alive, slowly converting the green wood into coal. Add wood as needed, and keep a watchful eye that the fire doesn't flare up too much—and burn your smokehouse down!

Smoke can also be used as a simple insect deterrent while drying meat in the sun. Hang your meat on a framework above a small, smoky fire. Again, don't let the fire cook your meat, just lightly smoke it and drive away flies and wasps while it dries.

Aging
Meat has traditionally been, and continues to be to a large extent, aged before consumption. The aging process can vary in length from two days to two months depending on conditions and the tastes and needs of the chef. Aging changes meat in two main ways. Enzymes present in the meat break down connective tissue in the muscle fibers, making the meat more

digestible and tender, with these qualities growing the longer the meat is aged. The enzymes actually predigest the meat for us. Aging meat also results in richer flavors.

To age meat, it is hung somewhere relatively cool, fly-free and well ventilated, with air freely flowing around the hanging sections. These sections could be whole legs, or single large muscles. The warmer it is, the faster meat ages. Modern meat aging takes place in coolers just a few degrees above freezing temperature, and takes from 15–28 days. I have hung deer legs for several weeks in an unheated cabin in the fall where the temperature probably fluctuated between 5 to 15 degrees Celsius, and the meat was tender and delicious. In hot summer weather, meat may only be able to hang a few days in the shade before it gets really aged. A greenish scum will typically form on the surface of aging meat; this is harmless and can be scraped off before eating. Some hunters prefer to age their kill with the skin left on for this reason, so no scum will form on the surface. Aging is somewhat of a short-term preservation method, but still very valuable and one that enhances nutrients much like fermentation.

Burying

What can you do if you have too much meat to eat, but no way to preserve it all and it's way too hot out to hang it to age for any length of time? Bury it! Meat will be able to age very slowly if you bury it a couple of feet down in a high, dry spot. Leave the skin on if you can, it will protect the meat from dirt and losing juices. I have buried a whole rabbit this way, with the guts left in and skin on (following a recipe in Bill Mollisson's *The Permaculture Book of Ferment and Human Nutrition*) for a couple of weeks in the heat of summer. I lined the bottom of the pit with leaves, plopped the rabbit in, covered it thickly with leaves and piled the earth back on. After two weeks of aging the rabbit was great. I skinned, gutted and made a stew with it—the meat was super tender! Had I tried to hang it, the rabbit would have been covered in maggots or broken down by bacteria and aged to mush by that time. You could bury whole deer legs like this and put heavy objects over the pits to keep scavengers out. Bury meat deeply enough to ensure it is below the zone of active, meat-eating insects (12-plus inches). As with hanging meat in the air to age, enzymes will predigest the meat when it is buried, making it more tender and digestible.

Rendering Fat

Rendering fat means separating pure oil from protein. This is done by taking animal fat and melting the oil out of the tissue using heat one of two ways—dry rendering or wet rendering. For dry rendering, cut the fat into bite-sized chunks. Place the chunks in a pot, with plenty of room to stir them around, and put over a low heat. The key here is to be careful. When the fat is just getting going you need to stir it fairly often to keep it from sticking and burning. Once enough oil has rendered that there is a nice amount of liquid fat at the bottom of the pot, you can relax a bit with your stirring. But still move it around regularly. The fat is done rendering when the bite-sized chunks you put in have shriveled and become crisp. Pour the hot oil off (not into plastic!) and store in a cool place. Hard fats (deer, bison, cow, goat, sheep and other ruminant animals) last longer if they can breathe. Don't put a lid on them unless they are stored very cold.

And those leftover crispy chunks are craquelins, quite a tasty snack; they are pretty much pork rinds.

Wet rendering is accomplished by putting chunks of fat (or bones, or whatever else has a high oil content you want to render) in a pot of water, bringing it to a low simmer for a few hours, and then allowing it to cool. Once fully cooled, the oil will rise to the top and solidify—skim it off and put it on a low heat to remove residual moisture if you want it to keep longer. Rendered bone marrow is quite the superfood.

Storing Fat

Pure oil or rendered fat from animal sources can usually be stored for many months without going rancid. Two factors cause it to spoil: bacteria and oxidation. Bacteria can only spoil rendered fat if it hasn't actually been rendered properly—that is, if there is residual water that wasn't removed from the fat while rendering. Properly rendered fat will have no moisture content; it is pure oil, and as such is pretty well ground zero for bacteria (which need moisture to exist). Leave rendered fat uncovered, especially while cooling, to allow any excess moisture to evaporate, and store it in a dry place.

Oxidation can be slowed by storing oils in a cool, dark place. Tallows (hard fats, usually from ungulates) are the most stable of animal fats (and possibly any food oil), keeping several months (two to six, depending on temperature and storage) before going rancid. Lards (semi-soft fats, usually from omnivores) are only slightly less stable, while liquid oils (fish, marine mammal or plant-sourced oils) are the least stable. One method I have discovered for longer-term preservation of rendered fat, transforming its shelf life from months to years, is canning. I know, canning isn't sustainable, but this information is obscure and useful enough that I'm including it. It's as simple as pouring boiling hot, freshly rendered fat into sterile jars, putting a lid and ring on and walking away. I'm guessing that canning improves storability by keeping the oil out of contact with oxygen. Oil canned this way will keep three years, possibly more. Botulism is apparently not of concern because it needs water to thrive and this is just oil.

Simply pour hot (boiling temperature) rendered fat into sterilized jars, leaving one half to three quarters of an inch headroom. Put a proper canning lid on the jar (having first soaked it in hot, near-boiling water) and fasten with a steel ring. Sit around and listen for a "pop" sound if you want to feel satisfied, otherwise allow it to sit overnight, letting the fat cool, then check the seal.

Pemmican

A staple food for indigenous peoples of the North American Plains, as well as many others elsewhere, pemmican consists of pulverized, dried red meat mixed with rendered fat. On the Plains both of these would traditionally have come from bison. Pemmican is a near perfect food. It has high-quality fat and protein in balance with one another, with dried berries, plants or seaweeds added to further enhance its nutritional value. It was also used as a staple food by pioneers and soldiers in the American West, where it was reputed to be the only food that a hard-working man could live off solely and still thrive indefinitely. I have personally eaten it as a staple food for months. For me, it is a heavenly food—a wild, nutrient-dense bread substitute. Of course it is a food of ecological affluence; only someone living in a healthy ecosystem rich with large ruminants could gather the raw materials for pemmican from the wild.

As an interesting side note, pemmican probably provides about 80 percent of its calories as fat. Usually highly saturated tallow or even more highly saturated suet (intestinal fat) is used. When I read that the traditional diet of many Inuit groups, as well as that of the pemmican-eating Plains people, provided 80 percent of their calories from fat, I was at first shocked. Modern conventional nutritionists recommend a diet of 20 percent calories from fat, little or none of which should be saturated. Upon reflection, though, I realized I had already eaten a diet with that ratio of calories from fat, pemmican having served as my staple for months on end. And no, I did not get fatter, in fact I was displeased with how *lean* I was, though I felt extremely healthy and energetic.

Pemmican can be made from any dried lean meat: deer, bison, cow, chum salmon, moose, goat, etc. Tallow from any of these creatures is ideal as the fat component, intestinal fat (suet) being the best. Dried berries are optional, and adding a sweetener would be sacrilege.

To make pemmican, first pulverize dried meat using a mortar and pestle or suitable substitute. Alternatively, if you have access to one, put dried meat in a food processor and grind to a powder. Put this pulverized meat into a large bowl, and if dried berries are going to be added, add them now.

Melt the rendered fat. Once it has liquefied completely—make sure it is just warm, not too hot—begin pouring it into the pulverized meat, stopping to mix it in, slowly adding more and mixing until the mixture can be formed into balls that stick together. Adding fat that is too hot will cook the meat and cause spoilage; make sure you can hold a finger in the fat to the count of ten. Once you can form balls or clumps, you can stop adding fat and either pack the pemmican into a jar or similar container, or form it into golf-ball-sized balls and store it away in these snack-sized chunks. Pemmican would traditionally be stored in rawhide containers known as "parfleche." I have stored it in both paper bags and buckskin pouches for nearly a year without spoilage. Containers of glass, plastic, plant fiber (provided it stays dry), wood or skin would all suffice.

A pemmican ball.

Sources often claim pemmican will last decades; I have kept it for a year, and it was still good eating. Decades I'm not sure about. Perhaps using smoked meat would enable pemmican to keep that long? In any case it is so delicious I won't be able to conduct that trial without eating it prematurely.

CHAPTER 15

Meet Your New Friends: Indispensable Plant Allies for Hard Times

M OST OF US reared in the industrialized world are starting from scratch when it comes to country skills that
were not long ago common folk knowledge. Without guidance
this can be overwhelming in almost every area. With plant
medicine, the plant books for your region might list hundreds
of useful wild species to learn. Many beginning students in
these endangered arts develop what some have dubbed "the
shaman complex." That is, they try to learn all of the potentially useful medicinal plants possible in their area, all at once,
to develop an encyclopedic knowledge. In reality, one can get
by quite well with the help of about half a dozen major plants
for most common medical needs from colds to sprains. Traditionally, common folk would (and do) know these plants well
and keep them close to home. The following are some of the
most significant, widespread, abundant folk medicine plants.
My intention here is not to offer advice as a skilled herbalist,
but rather to share common folk knowledge that all country
people should have in order to take care of themselves and
each other.

Comfrey (Symphytum Officinale)

The old country name for comfrey is "knitbone," which should give some clues as to how it is used medically. For healing sprains, fractures, bruising or other physical trauma, comfrey works wonders. Modern science has validated folk wisdom by isolating the constituent allantoin, a cell proliferant found in comfrey that speeds up the natural replacement of body cells. Both root and leaf are used, though the root has stronger medicinal properties, and since this is a plant often used in serious situations, strength often matters.

Comfrey is generally applied topically, as a liniment (alcohol extract or tincture), poultice (a slightly cooked mash of the root) or salve to a traumatized or sore area. Situations that would call for the use of comfrey include: a sprained ankle, a sore knee or other joint, severe bruising, broken or fractured bones. I often apply it to a sore shoulder, knee or any other joint that is aching from being bent too far in the wrong direction.

The only cautions with using comfrey are when there is an open, potentially infected wound. Its ability to stimulate cell reproduction can cause a wound to heal over too fast, trapping an infection inside it.

When harvesting, make sure you identify the plant properly—it has a resemblance to the extremely poisonous digitalis (foxglove). Harvesting when the plant is in flower is one way to accomplish this, as the flowers are purple and distinct. Otherwise fall is the best time. Roots can be grated or sliced thin and dried. This way, a poultice can be easily made by putting a bit of dry root in a pot with just enough water to turn it into a goopy mash. This is applied warm to the injured area by wrapping the mush in sterile cloth (just boil it) and using this like a gooey ice pack.

There is some controversy over whether or not comfrey

should be taken internally; it has been shown to cause cancerous cell growth in lab experiments. Those in the yes camp say that comfrey should only be used in acute situations, and its benefits in those times outweigh any slight addition to our carcinogenic load. It can be very useful with internal bleeding or other injuries. I have never used comfrey internally, so cannot give advice. Get to know the plant, do your homework and decide.

Yarrow (Achille Millefolium)

This plant has so many important medical applications it is mind boggling: it is antiseptic, haemostatic (stops bleeding), a circulatory stimulant, can kill influenza and the common cold dead, is diaphoretic (induces sweating) and even a deodorant.

This is a plant that has been taken to the battlefield to dress wounds for millennia. It is indispensable to any medicine shelf.

Yarrow for Wounds

Yarrow stops bleeding, is antiseptic and slightly analgesic (painkilling), making it an ideal wound dressing. For slices to the skin, knife cuts, shallow gashes, burns and scrapes, fresh yarrow leaves can be chewed into a spit poultice which is applied directly to the wound, tied on with a piece of cloth (leaves, buckskin, whatever you have—ideally this would be clean). This will help arrest bleeding and purify the wound of pathogenic bacteria. A yarrow wound powder can be made by crushing dried leaves into a powder. This is applied directly to shallow wounds—blood and the powder will mix and form a strong scab together.

For deep wounds, introducing plant material is usually contraindicated—a tea (infusion) can be made from yarrow flower blossoms and leaf and squirted into deep wounds or punctures as an antiseptic wash. Use a plastic syringe or improvise (a plastic bag with a small hole poked into it works). Add salt to further its effectiveness.

Yarrow and Influenza

Yarrow has the extraordinary ability to stop a flu or cold in its tracks at the onset of symptoms. The key being that it is taken *at the onset of symptoms*, when you start getting a sore throat, feeling achy, etc. The treatment is a strong yarrow blossom infusion. Take a handful of dried (or fresh) flower blossoms and pour a quart of hot, just boiled water over them. Cover and let steep 15 minutes. Drink hot and often and symptoms should subside.

Other Uses

Yarrow blossom tea induces sweating for any situation where that is indicated. It is a bitter digestive tonic, though it should not be taken consecutively for over two weeks because it is mildly toxic and hard on the liver. It can bring on menstruation and quell postpartum bleeding. It stimulates peripheral circulation, which brings more blood to the penis or clitoris, and can thus assist sexual arousal.

Wild Carrot/Queen Anne's Lace (Daucus Carota)

Wild carrot (also known as Queen Anne's lace) is a widespread Eurasian "weed." Its seeds have been used for millennia (the earliest written records date back to the 4th century bc) as an "implantation inhibitor"—a substance that stops a fertilized egg from implanting itself on a woman's uterine wall. If an egg cannot lodge onto the uterine wall, it cannot survive. It will disintegrate and menstruation will arrive as usual. In other words, wild carrot seeds have been traditionally (and are still) used as a natural morning-after pill. The herb is still in use today, and has documentation to support its effectiveness (see sisterzeus.com).

Its use requires that you are charting your cycle and know when you are going to ovulate or are ovulating. I cannot begin to cover this subject (charting fertility, etc.) fully, but here is a very incomplete synopsis; you should do a lot of homework before trying it.

Wild carrot works best as a morning after type of contraceptive. The big advantage to this is that it can be used as needed. The first dose should be taken within eight hours of being exposed to sperm, followed by another dose or two as needed. It can also be used in tincture form, which eliminates the need to chew the seeds.

Wild carrot seems to fail most for women who have just come off the pill or use it throughout their entire cycle, who have recently given birth or have experienced some other event that interferes with their natural hormonal balance and therefore the ability to know when ovulation is occurring.

Mature seed is harvested from seed heads in the fall. It can be dried in paper bags or on screens. *Wild carrot has several highly poisonous relatives, make sure you have positively identified it before harvesting!* Once you do know it, it is very easy to identify. Its big white flowers have a distinctive purple dot in their center. A year's worth of seed for you and your friends can be harvested in half an hour.

Take one teaspoon (five milliliters), chewed well and swallowed with water, within eight hours of unprotected penetrative sex with internal ejaculation near ovulation. Taking this herb routinely throughout the entire cycle reduces its effectiveness.

Plantain (Plantago Major and Plantago)

This plant was at one time called "white man's footprints," as nearly everywhere that Western civilization has spread, plantain has come along for the ride. It is used in the treatment of wounds (like comfrey it contains allantoin, but it has no toxic side effects), insect bites, bronchitis and hemorrhoids. Plantain disinfects, speeds healing, reduces pain and soothes.

For bee stings, small burns and cuts and scrapes, plantain, which can be found growing in amongst the grasses, is chewed up and applied as a spit poultice for instant pain relief, to cleanse, stop bleeding (it acts as a coagulant) and speed recovery.

With hemorrhoids, fresh plantain can be chewed well and swallowed (or if only the dry plant is available, taken as an infusion). Its soothing, healing abilities act directly on the hemorrhoids as it passes through the colon and anus.

A strong plantain infusion is very helpful for dry, hoarse coughs. I have many friends who have cured themselves of serious bronchitis using this plant to soothe and heal their poor lungs.

The Tanners

No, I'm not talking about everyone's favorite 1990s television family, I'm talking about plants that contain large amounts of tannic acid (tannin). Tannin is a bitter, astringent plant compound that binds to proteins. The term tannin is derived from tanning leather, a process that has traditionally used tannins to turn fresh, perishable skins into durable leather by binding tannin to protein (dead skin in this case). Tannins have antibacterial, antiviral and antiparasitic properties. They can be used to stop diarrhea. Some of the best sources of tannin are the barks of oak, hemlock, alder, spruce, fir, birch, aspen and yellow or red dock root. Together these plants inhabit much of the temperate world. Green and black teas contain tannin, that is what makes them astringent and bitter.

Tanning Burns

The ability of tannins to tighten and toughen skin makes them very useful in the treatment of burns. They bind to the raw, exposed proteins, making them tighten up and giving strength in the same way they transform raw skins into leather. In World War I, the use of pure tannic acid to treat burn wounds—whether caused by incendiary bombs, mustard gas or lewisite—significantly reduced mortality rates. When pure tannic acid was not available, strong lukewarm tea was substituted.

Tannin is applied to burns and scalds directly either as a strong liquid extract (tea) or using dressings soaked in strong tannin-rich tea. To make such a tea using bark, typically the most available and richest source of tannin, chop the bark as finely as you have the patience to. Fill a pot half full with it and cover with water nearly to the top. Bring to a low simmer and brew for 20 minutes to an hour. Bark harvested in spring has the highest tannin content and will peel more easily, though it is useable at all times of the year. For dock root, make a decoction similarly, but with half as much plant material to water as for bark.

Tannin Wash

A tannin-rich tea, as noted above, makes an excellent all-purpose disinfectant. It can be used as a hand wash, to clean counters and anywhere one wants to use a sterilizing cleaner. It is sometimes used as a mouthwash as well—the only hitch being that most tannin teas you make will have a strong color and are very effective dyes; they will stain your teeth. Keep this in mind when using tannin as a cleansing wash.

The Berbers

"Berbers" refers to a group of plants that contain a compound called berberine. Goldenseal, Oregon grape, and barberry are the most well known, widespread members of this clan. My experience lies primarily with Oregon grape, as I live intimately with it, so I will primarily talk about it here. Keep in mind that the main active compound in Oregon grape root is berberine, and so its actions and applications are very similar to the other Berbers.

Among its other properties, Oregon grape root is antibacterial, antiviral, antifungal, antiparasitic, a gall bladder stimulant and a liver cleanser. It is used as an effective treatment for giardia, herpes, systemic fungal infections (candida) and blood poisoning, as a strong liver tonic to aid the liver in cleansing and improving nutrient absorption, to fend off the common cold and for many other conditions. The part used is the root bark, which apparently contains strong medicine throughout the whole year, though some prefer to harvest it in the fall (I don't). The bark is simply scraped off with a knife or whatever you have — it should be bright yellow, this is the medicine you want.

A general-use tea is prepared by gently decocting (simmering) the root bark in water. I use a palmful of root bark to a liter of water decocted for 15-plus minutes. After pouring off the brew, the plant matter may be rebrewed a couple of times, a bit longer with each successive brewing. The decoction will be a deep yellow-orange colour and have a strong bitter flavor.

For Giardia

Oregon grape is an effective treatment and preventive for giardia, a parasite that can bring on diarrhea, excess gas, stomach or abdominal cramps, upset stomach and nausea. Treatment consists of taking strongly brewed Oregon grape tea in two-cup doses, every six hours in acute conditions and once or twice daily in chronic conditions for many weeks, until symptoms clear and then continue for one or more weeks to prevent a relapse. Oregon grape's berberine is somewhat less available than that in goldenseal, and so is safer to use long term. Taken as a regular tonic, Oregon grape can prevent giardia by creating an uninhabitable environment for it in the guts.

For Infections

The tea is used both internally and externally in the treatment of severe infections (leading to blood poisoning or septicemia). An example would be an infected cut on the finger, which has become very inflamed with red streaks moving up the hand towards the arm, indicating serious, potentially systemic, blood poisoning. A strong Oregon grape decoction can be taken internally, one to two liters daily, and the infected area immersed in hot (as hot as can be tolerated) Oregon grape tea. Soak the infected region in strong, hot Oregon grape for one hour every six hours for the first day, and continue soaking at least every twelve hours, as well as taking the tea internally for a week or more until all symptoms have cleared.

CHAPTER 16

Feral Food Cultivation: Thoughts and Strategies on "Tending the Wild"

"FERAL CULTIVATION"—these two words aren't usually used together, and if they are, they are in conflict. In recent years anthropologists and the sustainability movement have been abuzz with the rediscovered phenomenon that indigenous, hunter-gatherer cultures everywhere seem to have cultivated their food sources in ways that were invisible to their civilized conquerors. Hunter-gatherers in the Pacific Northwest carefully tended berry patches (pruning, coppicing, fertilizing and transplanting them), routinely burned the understory of mature forests to enhance forage for elk and deer, and established estuarine root gardens over generations. Elders recall people in the old days establishing salmon in creeks where they were absent by planting fertilized eggs in their gravel banks. Extensive camas plots were carefully tended, fertilized and weeded in oak meadows. In other parts of the world, what appeared to be wild jungle forests to European newcomers were in fact carefully tended, semi-feral forest gardens. To Western academics these findings are surprising, but in reality, one would assume that any culture living sustainably in a bioregion for millennia would have a symbiotic, beneficial relationship with its food sources. In the same way that a good lover is sensitive to what turns their partner on and gets them off, a good creature is sensitive to its host's, the land's, signals. All successful species enhance the health of their host; sane humans are no different.

Cultivation vs. Domestication

We've already looked at some of the downfalls of domestication, how it is synonymous with unsustainable growth, ecological degradation and oppressive class structures. The theme of this book is rewilding, moving in the opposite direction from domestication, so the question is: Where do we draw the line between cultivation and domestication? When do we cross the line between gently supporting our food sources and completely dominating, controlling and degrading a land base? This question is enormously important.

While domestication involves domination — suppression of unwanted species and tight control over those desired, creating species and habitats that are completely human-dominated — cultivation means supporting selected species in much more subtle ways. People of the Northwest coast traditionally broke branches off blueberry and huckleberry plants after or during harvest as a form of pruning to keep the plants in a state of heavy production. It is well known that black bears of the Northwest coast do this also, breaking off branches during harvest to keep berry bushes productive. Cultivation is neither inherently destructive nor uniquely human. Sometimes it is simply a by-product of harvesting.

In fact, the simple act of harvesting can often enhance the health of plant and animal communities. Many friends and acquaintances have noted that in the spots where they harvest nettles yearly, the nettles continue to grow tall and robustly, while in spots where they do not harvest, the nettles have shorter lives, giving way to the next phase in succession more quickly. Harvesting can slow or freeze succession, the rate at which one plant community gives way to another species (from thistle and grass to salmonberry and alder to cedar and salal, for example).

Selectively harvesting root plants for food allows the plants left behind more elbow room to fatten up. The implications and possibilities of this concept are huge; most any healthy community of plants and animals will benefit from intelligent harvesting.

Perception

When "food" is only something that is culturally approved, something that *we* "grow," as opposed to what the land provides when left to itself, we are at war with the land. We are at war with wildness.

For example, in the city of Victoria, Canada, and in many towns and cities across North America, there is growing concern about the "deer problem." Deer populations have blossomed in many suburban and urban areas as a result of increased habitat (manicured lawns, clearings) and a decrease in human and non-human predation. Meanwhile over 11 million acres of genetically modified canola are under cultivation in Canada alone. Why hasn't anyone been talking about the "canola problem"? Really, it's taking over! That's 11 million acres and growing of canola monoculture.

Of course the answer is that this culture values canola as food; deer, not so much. Or perhaps, and this might be at the root of it, *anything* wild, not so much. I'm not saying that a deer overpopulation doesn't harm the land, but it is only a "problem" because we don't see deer as food—we're not eating them or allowing other predators to.

So this is the delicate dance we need to learn—how to live in the hands of the gods (the land), to erase the destructive programming that would have us dam a salmon-spawning river so we can grow soybeans. How to elegantly enhance food sources that make sense, and make use of those that don't need any enhancement. My thought is that the most developed cultures are those that have the most seamless relationship with their land base. They are so good at tending their gardens that you can't even see them.

The principle is the same as the Buddhist *Ahimsa*: do no unnecessary harm.

Practice

As a practical matter, this path has several levels. One is to learn how to appreciate what the land is already offering—getting acquainted with wild edibles. This first step, unprogramming, is essential for living on the land in a healthy way.

Another level is learning how to support plant and animal communities that can feed us in a way that is actually sustainable, elegant, gentle and effective. This might look like planting resilient, non-native species in disturbed sites, heavily pruning a berry patch every few years to increase fruiting, harvesting things in an intentional way or, for the adventurous (and skilled!), controlled burns to enhance a food-producing understory and create browse for deer.

One of the most significant, beneficial ways a human can support the land is simply by living on it—pissing and shitting on it. Our bodies excrete dense fertility daily that, if we put it back into the land where we live, has tremendous effects on plant growth and soil health.

What follows is an incomplete assortment of notes, tips and ideas that may be helpful. It's not a complete guide by any stretch, but includes some valuable tactics that can help you begin looking at things differently.

Proper Harvesting

- Learn how to harvest plants sustainably. This means only harvesting from areas where there is a healthy population of a given species, and as a general rule, harvesting no more than ten percent of what is there. Sites slated for imminent development are exceptions—harvest all you need in such situations.
- Root vegetables get bigger if they are thinned out by harvesting. Jerusalem artichoke, camas and many others should be harvested by thinning, or completely harvested and then some of the harvest replanted with plenty of space between plants.
- Almost all plants and animals grow more vigorously when they are thinned out by selective harvesting. As mentioned above, intelligent harvesting is a kind of cultivation.
- Avoid breaking off the fruit spur when harvesting crab-apples, wild and cultivated apples and other pome fruits.
- Harvesting salal berries by picking off the whole fruiting stem encourages the growth of more fruiting stems in following years.
- One male can impregnate many females. When hunting any animal population that isn't robust, go for the guys.
- Adult male deer, along with many other creatures, will have the most fat in early fall, before mating season. This is the most intelligent time to harvest them, you will get the most calories out of your kill.
- Get to know what you are harvesting. Live in a place for a few years, come back to the same harvesting grounds and see what effect you are having, how the community you are

taking from is responding to your activities. See how they respond to different things.

Cultivation Strategies

A pile of leaves and other decomposable debris, once it has rotted down a bit, becomes an excellent spot to plant feral root vegetables like burdock, wild carrot, dandelion, etc. It provides plenty of organic matter for those roots to dig deep in and be pulled out of easily.

Many food producing trees and shrubs respond well to **coppicing**—being cut down to the trunk and left to regrow. I live near a town that early colonists planted densely with hazelnut trees, many of which are still producing in abundance (the lucky ones that got through). I have noticed that nearly all of them appear to have been cut back to a trunk at some point. Coppicing seems to "set back the clock" so to speak: a tree that would otherwise be long past its productive years can be set back to the vigor of young adulthood by cutting it back and letting it regrow. I have seen pictures of a 1,000-year-old lime tree that has been repeatedly coppiced. It is still thriving, and has probably lived centuries longer and produced far more biomass than it would have if never touched. Indigenous peoples in many areas would cut back berry bushes periodically, when they outgrew their peak phase of productivity, to set back the clock. One also harvests wood as a result of coppicing; it is often used as a method of managing timber. Coppiced trees regenerate biomass far more quickly than trees starting from scratch.

Permaculturists often make use of **swales**, gentle ditches dug at right angles to the slope of a piece of land. Swales slow and disperse rainfall runoff as it travels along the surface of land, significantly increasing the infiltration of rainwater into soil and preventing soil erosion. If you are living in an area that has been cleared, this could be a wise method of terraforming to consider before the earth is once again covered. In arid areas swales can actually facilitate the regrowth of vegetation where there otherwise wouldn't be any. All you need is a shovel and some time. Mini-swales can be easily dug around fruit and nut trees to help them capture as much rainwater as possible.

Iroquois gardeners, among others, traditionally seeded cleared ground with seedballs—balls of clay, soil or compost, and seeds. Encasing the seeds in clay keeps the seeds safe from predators until they germinate, which will be whenever it rains and the seedball becomes sufficiently moist. Seedballs are easy to make and use. Here's a recipe that requires red powdered clay (terracotta clay—friends have been given buckets of this stuff by pottery suppliers that said it had been ruined by over-heating but was still good for seedballs), humus soil or compost, seeds and water.

Combine five parts powdered red clay, three parts soil and one part seeds (choose resilient plants: burdock, kale, radishes, whatever you like that is somewhat hardy) in a large container. Add the seeds last.

Spray or dribble water into the mixture while stirring; add just enough that it sticks together. Form into small pennysized balls and let them dry in the sun.

Members of the *ribes* family (currants) have a tenacious ability to root. Cut shoots or branches off established plants during the dormant months, jam them into the soil and they will likely root and start a new life on their own. Willow is also a tenacious rooter capable of growing from cuttings jammed into the ground, for weavers or living-fence makers.

Sites of old burn piles and other areas recently disturbed by fire are usually highly fertile. The recycling of minerals into soil is sped up by the ash, which also changes the pH of the soil to something most European vegetables are more used to.

Recent burn sites are great spots to experiment seeding feral veggies.

Experimenting with these concepts gives a very literal meaning to "listening to the land." That is what we need to do, to listen and watch and step into another level of awareness of how we interact with the physical world.

CHAPTER 17

Hunter-Gatherer, Gardener-Trapper

I NDIGENOUS CULTURES often employ the most elegant, efficient means to harvest a given food. Massive fish weirs and
traps in rivers of the Pacific Northwest are a testament to this.
With these weirs in place salmon could be effortlessly harvested during their spawning runs upriver. They simply swam
en masse into the trap, where they could be easily scooped up
with a simple dip net, clubbed, gutted and preserved. There is
little "sport" to this method of fishing, but when you are trying to feed a village, not prove something to yourself or others,
sport is not much of a consideration.

Instead of spending hours and days stalking the woods
in search of deer, many indigenous hunters would set tough
snares made from sinew, rawhide or other suitable material
on well-traveled deer trails. This way they could be out doing
whatever else they needed to (gather firewood, tell stories, care
for a loved one, check the fish traps) and still passively harvest
deer for food. Again, not as sportsmanlike, but more effective. Trapping was and is an enormous part of life for people
that depend on wild animals for their subsistence. Some cultures that are labeled as "hunter-gatherers" might in truth be

something more akin to "gardener-trappers"—cultivating and enhancing specific plant (and, in subtle ways, animal) communities for food, and using trapping as a primary means of, well, hunting.

Trapping has many advantages over hunting with projectile weapons. It is a passive form of harvest, meaning one quickly sets the trap and leaves, instead of staying in place until the prey comes along (*if* it comes along). Also, hunting with projectile weapons has a hitch: one might simply wound the prey, or worse, kill it but not be able to find it after it has completed its final sprint. Traps, properly set, have a much lower likelihood of losing or injuring prey.

Knowing how to use (and make) projectile weapons is incredibly valuable, and often the only legal way to harvest many creatures. Trapping, however, is in many instances the most effective and elegant way of harvesting creatures for food. In any situation where one is depending solely on the land for their survival, trapping is essential. Some of the following traps could be set in minutes by seriously sick, injured or otherwise compromised individuals, making harvesting animal food a viable option where otherwise it would not be.

Ethically, trapping is a contentious issue. Many animal rights advocates vehemently condemn the trapping of animals as cruel and inhumane. Nowadays, of course, trapping is not typically a subsistence activity, it is a profit-driven industry where huge amounts of creatures are killed for their furs, their bodies thoughtlessly discarded. Used as a sane subsistence activity, properly set traps kill instantly or near instantly, as well as securing the kill in place so that it may be easily retrieved and fully used. Set and used correctly, traps are absolutely humane and ethical—I'm not talking about steel legholds here.

What follows are some general guidelines to follow in subsistence and survival trapping, as well as a handful of highly effective traps for specific creatures that I or others I know have used successfully.

On the Trapline

Where hunting is based on stealth, trapping is based on deception. When one sets a trap, they want their prey to think nothing is out of the ordinary, nothing is alarming or dangerous about the area where the trap is set. There are a few ways one can deceive their prey to this end:

Study your prey. Find out as much as possible about any creature you intend to trap or hunt. What do they eat? Where do they like to sleep? When are they most active? When do they mate? When do they raise their young? What do their tracks look like when they're running, walking, feeding? Children's animal books are often excellent resources for this kind of information. By learning about your prey you will be more effective in harvesting it for food, as well as having a deeper understanding and appreciation of it.

Eliminate your scent. Most non-human animals have a much more acute sense of smell than we do, and use it as a constant means of communication and information gathering. If your scent is smeared all over an area, creatures will know a human has been there and will exercise caution. If you have set a trap with your scent-covered hands, they are going to be extra careful and know something is up. Cover your scent by smoking your clothing or storing it with aromatic conifer boughs (cedar, fir, pine—whatever grows in your area), rubbing charcoal, ash or aromatic plants, local to the area you are trapping, on your hands and likewise descenting your footwear. Rubber boots are said to shed scent more readily than other materials, making them a good candidate for hunting or trapping foot gear. Buckskin clothing has the advantage of always being pre-smoked. Do not walk in areas people have urinated on with your hunting shoes, and avoid getting your own urine on them or any other hunting garb (as well as any possible hunting or trapping areas).

Check your traps once a day. Check your traps once a day, in the morning. Many non-human creatures are most active at dusk and dawn, meaning your traps will likely catch something right before it gets dark, or right when it's getting light out. Checking your traps less than once a day is bad form; if a creature has been trapped but not killed it is needlessly suffering. If you have set traps, it is your responsibility to check them daily and ensure anything you catch passes on as swiftly as possible.

Check them from a distance. Avoid recontaminating the trapping area with your scent by checking traps visually from as far away as you can; don't go right up to them unless you need to.

Trap in the spring, fall and winter. These seasons are better than summer, if you have the luxury of choice, the main reason being that during a hot spell, when the temperature barely dips below 30 degrees, anything you trap will, like roadkill, quickly begin degrading. The larger the creature, the more rapidly this process gets under way. Not the end of the world, but not ideal.

Be an astute observer. Pay attention to any signals and signs your prey gives you. If your trap is knocked down but empty, try to deduce why. Was it set too high? Too low? Was it just the wind? Was it another creature? *Constant observation, awareness* *and adjustment are essential.* As you set and check your traps, you are a predator. Step into that role fully, taking in information and embodying the cunning and stealth of a cougar who was born in a human body and so uses traps instead of tooth and claw.

Know the law. Some types of traps are legal, some aren't. Some creatures can be trapped legally any time, some cannot be legally trapped except in emergency survival conditions. Know what the law is where you live, regardless of how you intend to act in relation to it.

Snares

Snares are traps that use a noose to either kill or hold a creature in place. For many creatures and situations they are the most practical, effective and easily set trap. The basic premise behind snares is that a creature puts its head (or leg or paw) through a noose, which then tightens either by the creature's own pulling or by a trigger mechanism that, when tripped, puts tension on the noose. The following are some variations of the snare for various creatures.

The Basic Snare

The most basic variation of the snare is simply a noose hung across a given creature's trail, anchored to a sapling along the side so that when a creature walks along it becomes ensnared around the neck, attempts to break free by pulling and breaks its own neck or chokes.

In areas where native rabbits have established runs, rabbit snares are typically set like this, using strong cordage or the modern favorite, thin brass or stainless steel wire.

Such a snare should be about a fist in diameter, and have its bottom raised four finger widths above ground. Adjust these

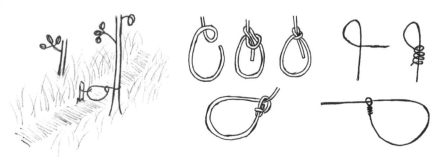

Rabbit snare set on established run.

Bowline knot used for snare.

How to fashion wire into a snare.

measurements as the situation dictates. Snares made from wire will happily stay propped up in thin air; those made from cordage or string will need to be propped up by twigs or sticks.

In some areas rabbits do not have runs, particularly where they have been introduced or gone feral. In these instances a baited and triggered snare will prove more effective. A triggered snare is one possessing a mechanism that, when triggered, pulls and puts tension on the snare, catching the prey and either killing it instantly or holding the noose on taut.

A "spring" snare, set at the entrance to a baited pen made by driving sticks into the ground.

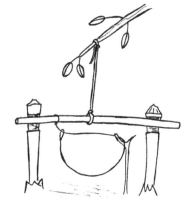

Close-up of the trigger mechanism. This is called a t-bar trigger. The horizontal stick, tied to a springy sapling or branch, is held in place by notches in the uprights.

The key here is to make the trigger touchy enough that it will spring at the slightest tug, but not so touchy that it will come apart as soon as you set it and walk away.

Survival Deer Snares

Snaring deer might sound desperate, cruel and extreme, but traditionally it was the primary method of harvesting for many groups of indigenous people. Properly set, a snare will kill a deer very quickly, and if the proper cord is used, there is little chance of losing one's kill. It is a passive method of harvest; setting a trap might take five minutes, after which the only work required is checking the trap daily, making it ideal for a survival situation where one's health and energy are compromised.

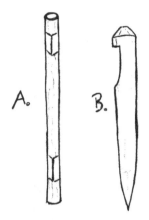

A is the horizontal piece, the edges of which are squared where it will come into contact with the notched uprights. B is the notched upright; two of these are driven into the ground solidly enough that they can hold while being tugged upwards by the sapling tied to A.

I learned of this method from a retired Survival, Evasion, Resistance, Escape (SERE) trainer—it is simply a scaled-up version of the basic snare described above, using a more elaborate knot.

First, find a deer trail. Then find a place on the deer trail with a tree growing right beside it. You can use this tree as the anchor for your snare. Make sure it is alive and solid enough that a deer will not be able to break or uproot it when pulling on the snare. Attach your noose to this tree. Military-grade parachute cord is often recommended because it has a tensile strength of 550 pounds and is as thin as a shoelace. Any cord of similar or greater strength can be used, provided it is limber enough to accomplish simple knots. Traditionally such snares would be made from reverse-wrapped sinew or twisted rawhide cord.

The noose is constructed using one simple, elegant knot: the Canadian jam hitch (see diagram). The reason this knot is used is that it is a non-relaxing knot, meaning it will tighten, but won't loosen. This means that if a deer gets caught it will not be able to shake the snare off, but will either choke itself to death or break its neck by jumping.

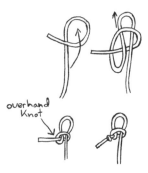

overhand knot

The Canadian jam hitch, a simple non-relaxing knot, is just a basic slip-knot jammed with an overhand knot.

Feed the free end of the cord through your jam hitch to form a noose; it should be 12–18 inches in diameter, bigger if you may be catching antlered deer. And from my source: "I always set the snare about crotch height with the bottom of the noose about knee height. I set it where deer can see it so they know where to put their head. As far as the deer suffering, every one I have caught hardly kicked up any leaves before expiring."

The snare can be anchored to the tree using any of your favorite tried-and-true knots. My source just used a slip knot followed by a couple of overhand knots.

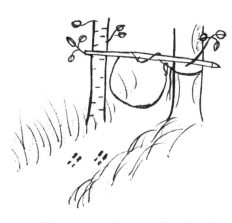

Deer snare set on a well-used trail, the noose being about 16 inches in diameter, the top crotch height, the bottom at knee level, tied off to a solid tree.

Even though mid- to late-winter isn't a period of high activity for deer, it's the only season where bucks don't have antlers and does aren't very pregnant, so if you happen to find yourself in a survival situation then it is still a good time of year for such a trap.

The Squirrel Pole Snare

This snare was widely used by nineteenth and twentieth century trappers. It can be used in deep coniferous woods or gardens with nut trees, wherever there are signs of squirrel habitation. In the woods look for middens—piles of nut shells or cone bracts that have accumulated over time near a squirrel's den.

A horizontal pole of one to one and a half-inch diameter is suspended between two trees, four to six feet above ground level. Traditionally the pole is held in place by nailing one end firmly into its supporting tree, and resting the other on a nail pounded into its supporting tree. This is so that during winds and weather the pole has some give and will not break easily.

Alternatives to nailing into trees would be resting one end on a branch and lashing the other using a strong natural (and camouflaged) material, or using hardwood pegs instead of nails. If you choose nails, find dead trees to nail into.

Snares are affixed to this pole, so that when squirrels run between trees their heads pass through a noose, the noose tightens, they are caught, jump off and hang. The small diameter of this pole is essential; a wider pole will give them room to run around the snares. Likewise, setting the snare noose at the proper height will ensure they don't jump over or glide under them. If using string or cord, your snares will need to be propped up with sticks; wire nooses will hold in place on their own.

This can be turned into a baited trap by attaching a bait container (a hollow tube that squirrels can fit through) to

Squirrel pole snare. The noose propped up with twigs is string or cord; wire nooses will hold in place on their own.

the middle of your horizontal pole. Good bait would be nuts and oily aromatic seeds, grains or chunks of bread.

I should mention that rat traps will also work on squirrels, though squirrels are very fast and wise, so expect to lose some bait if setting rat traps for them.

Mouse Traps

Mice (shrews, moles, voles, etc.) can be an important survival food, or an everyday fare if we need them to be. They often live in our homes, much to our dismay, and people end up killing them and throwing their dead bodies out, or relocating them if they are more sensitive. Mice are a source of valuable protein, fats and minerals that we barely have to get out of the house to harvest. Of course, they are potential hosts to hantavirus, a potentially lethal virus that is usually contracted when people are cleaning up cabins with mouse infestations. Sweeping up mouse droppings causes particles to become airborne—the person cleaning up inhales these and becomes infected. For this reason, mouse nests and poop should be handled with caution: wet down and mop up mouse poo instead of sweeping or vacuuming.

All that said, according to wilderness living expert John McPherson's probing of several health authorities, hantavirus is heat sensitive—cooking destroys it. So when consuming mice, there are two main precautions to take: cook them well, and handle them as little and as carefully as possible. There are a couple of ways I have heard of and experimented with for eating them.

First, simply skewer the dead mouse and roast it over coals. Don't bother skinning it. That would expose you unnecessarily to potential pathogens. Gutting is optional. It increases your risk and leaving the guts in is harmless, though it does affect the flavor depending on what the mouse has been eating. If you do gut your mice, disinfect your hands afterwards. The hair can be singed off by the heat of the coals, then the body cooked through. Eat the whole thing, bones and all—they are tiny and will crunch up in your mouth, a valuable source of calcium. If you are comfortable and confident enough, you can skin and gut mice before cooking. This will transform them from an awkward survival food into a delicious, crunchy little treat. Sautéed mice, if skinned and gutted, will have a delicious flavor, similar to squirrel. Folks at the Teaching Drum outdoor survival school do this, without much regard for hantavirus. I've been told that a fellow there is saving up mouse skins in hopes that one day in his old age he might be able to make himself a mouse-skin coat. Again, though, by handling their bodies you are increasing your exposure to any potential pathogen.

Another, more subtle approach for the faint of heart is to make a broth from whole mice. Just plop them into a pot of water, simmer for a couple of hours, strain and use as a nutritious base for soups, containing valuable minerals, fats and amino acids (protein).

As for traps, simple mouse traps work, of course. They are a wise addition to any survival kit. Another, more effective method is the old bucket trap. Fill a bucket or any other similar waterproof container with 5-plus inches of water. Put a buoyant float into the bucket (a piece of light wood, cork, etc.), with a piece of aromatic bait attached so that it is held above the water. A peg of harder wood, nail or needle driven into the float so that it sticks up, to which the bait is attached, works well. Place a ramp leading up to the edge of the bucket, and when a mouse smells the bait, it will run up the ramp, jump into the bucket and drown. Many

Mouse bucket trap; the mice hop in for good food, but drown.

mice a night may be caught using this trap; I have caught over a dozen overnight.

Deadfalls

Deadfalls are a class of traps where a trigger mechanism, when tripped, drops a heavy object on the prey, hopefully killing it swiftly. In most situations, deadfall traps are not as practical or effective as snares. Many survival books depict deadfalls set for large creatures such as deer and bear. The drawings and write-ups are convincing, until you try it for yourself. The killing weight that a deadfall drops on its prey must be three times the weight of the prey itself. This means a raccoon trap, assuming a raccoon could be up to 20 pounds in weight, would need a weight of somewhere around 60 pounds to be effective. Trying to balance a 60-pound weight on a deadfall trigger and still have the trigger touchy enough that it can be easily tripped is something akin to magic. And a deer might require over 500 pounds! Magic is, of course, real and part of life, so I have included a deadfall trap trigger here. Its most realistic applications are for smaller creatures and lightweight or cage traps.

The key here is to remember that the weight must be three times that of the intended prey, and that the trigger must hold in place well, yet be sensitive to the slightest touch in order to be effective. This particular deadfall is called "the Figure 4 Deadfall" because the pieces, when put together, create the shape of a "4."

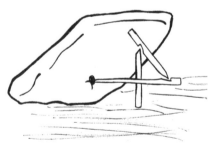

The Figure 4 Deadfall. When the baited end of the horizontal stick is moved, the trigger comes apart, dropping the weight on your prey.

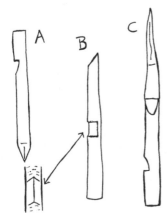

Components of the figure 4. A is carved to a flattened point on one end, notched near the other. B has one end flat, the other cut on a diagonal; a flattened edge is carved into it to lock into the notch on the horizontal bait stick. C is tapered to a point on one end to receive bait; it is also notched in two places to lock into the other trigger pieces.

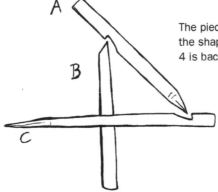

The pieces put together, to create the shape of a 4 (in this case the 4 is backwards).

CHAPTER 18

Dressing and
Undressing Our Food:
How to Skin and Gut a Creature

I CAN REMEMBER vividly the first time I gutted a deer. It
wasn't with my dad or uncle or grandfather, it was with
another friend who had never done it before. We'd been an-
ticipating it for quite some time, wanting to learn how to eat
the deer, raccoons and rabbits we regularly saw dead on the
roadside, how to eat wild meat from right where we lived. My
friend got a book called *Field Dressing Your Big Game*, filled
with detailed instructions and colour photographs depicting
the steps in gutting big game (deer, moose, elk, etc.). This and
the deer were our teachers.

Eventually we found a roadkilled deer, and it was time. After stashing the deer in a good secluded spot near the road,
we anticipated a lot of blood and gore, so we went and dumpstered some clothes so ours—though they were by no means
fancy—wouldn't get completely soaked in blood. We remem-
bered all the steps from the book, and were quite shocked
when we discovered how easy it was. And we only had blood
up to our wrists; we did not end up soaked in it as expected.

Since then I have gutted (or dressed) and skinned (un-
dressed) countless deer and other creatures. It's easy. Anyone

155

can do it. You quickly realize how long your ancestors have been doing this once you try it. To many it feels so natural, it's as though these actions are part of our cellular memory. Here is a brief description of the steps for a deer, since various species of deer are found throughout much of the world and the steps in gutting and skinning them apply to many other creatures, along with a few tips and tricks we have learned over the years. All you need is a sharp blade, or a dull one and some extra patience.

Dressing (Gutting)

Lay the deer on its back. You can keep the deer steady and propped in this position by using rocks, pieces of wood or whatever you have handy as blocks on either side of the body. We begin at the anus. Before you get into the guts, it's best to free the anus and colon. Cut the skin and tendons connecting them to the body so the colon will gently slide out with all the

Propping up the deer.

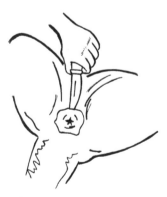

Cutting around (not into!)
the anus and colon.

Tying the anus closed after cutting the
tendons and tissues connecting the
anus and colon to their cavity.

other guts. Use your knife to carefully cut around it (not into it), until it will slide in and out of its nook.

Use a piece of string to tie it off at the end, so no poo can escape when you get around to pulling this out with the rest of the guts.

Pulling up paunch to make an incision.

Pinch some skin around the belly/paunch and pull it out. This way you can make a cut through this skin and membrane without cutting towards the guts and puncturing them. Make a cut through this pinched-up skin and membrane, until you can see the stomach that lies beneath them.

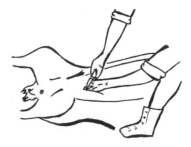

Making a cut through the paunch. Keep the blade from cutting downward and into the guts.

Now that you have made a point of entry, take your free hand and stick your fingers into it. Make it wider by tearing and prying with your fingers if you can. Now pull this opening up and away from the guts. Take your knife and, with the blade facing upwards (towards you, away from the guts), insert it into this hole, using your free hand to keep the skin (and knife) pulled taut, away from the guts.

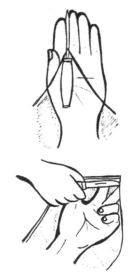

Now you are in a position to safely make an incision from the paunch all the way up to the rib cage. Keep the skin and connective tissue you are cutting through pulled away from the guts while you make this cut. Your free hand is at once pulling the skin away from the guts and keeping them pushed down, away from the blade.

Two methods of making a cut without puncturing the guts.

Cutting through
the sternum.

The cavity fully opened,
ready to cut the diaphragm
and remove the guts.

Pulling the guts out by
beginning with the windpipe.

This may sound hard, but it is really quite easy once you are doing it.

When you get to the rib cage you can do one of two things: stop cutting there and reach up into this cavity to pull the guts out, or cut through the rib cage up to the neck. I almost always do the latter. On most deer this can be done with the knife you are using. There is a soft cartilaginous spot just to either side of the breastbone. With a bit of finesse and some muscle power, you can find it and, keeping the knife from pointing down into the stomach, cut through the ribs and up to the base of the neck. If it's too hard with a knife, use a saw or don't bother.

Now you have opened the body cavity. The diaphragm is a muscle that separates the stomach, lower intestines and other organs from the lungs and heart which rest above. It is attached all around the cavity to the rib cage. You can cut it free at this point or cut and tear it free with your hands when pulling out all the guts.

Now cut the windpipe and esophagus where they come out of the neck. If you didn't cut through the ribs, you'll have to reach up and do this in the dark. Now pull down and out on the esophagus — all of the guts are linked to this so they will come with it.

Pull with one hand and use your knife with the other to cut any tissue attaching the gut bundle to the back. Once the diaphragm is out of the way, the stomach and intestines should pull out with a little coaxing. As you work you can remove any organs or fat you want to save.

Now the guts are all out, and if the anus has been properly freed it will come along with them. If it stays put, use your knife to disconnect it completely.

If you have done a clean job (and were starting with a clean kill) there won't be any stomach contents or poop left in the deer's cavity. Normally, though, there will be a pool of blood. You can save this by scooping it out with a container for eating fresh, cooked or dried. Blood coagulates almost instantly upon contact with oxygen, so much of this blood may be in coagulated blobs; it's still good, and even easier to collect.

Undressing (Skinning)

Skinning most herbivores is very easy. Once the initial cuts are made the skin can usually be pulled and pried off. Omnivorous creatures' skin is not as easily pulled off—a knife usually needs to be used to cut it off. These instructions are for deer, and apply to almost all herbivores.

If the weather is cool and you want to age your deer meat for a while, you can leave the skin on until you decide it's time to butcher.

It is easiest to skin a deer if it is hanging. This way you can get more leverage, the meat doesn't get dirty, and you can see what you are doing better. Hang a deer by its head (around the neck) or hind legs, and make your skinning cuts as depicted below.

Cut through skin and tendons to break off lower leg.

Make a slit on the back of the hind legs, just about the knee joint. There is a strong tendon there, and you can simply slide a pole through these holes to conveniently hang the deer.

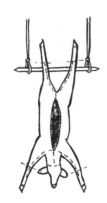

Deer hanging from
hind legs.

Make skinning cuts on the front of the front legs, where white and brown hair meet, and on the back of the hind legs, where white and brown hair meet. By placing the skinning cuts like so, the hide will have a more useable, square shape when removed.

Once the initial skinning cuts have been made, you can put down your knife. Peel and pry the skin away from the flesh until you can get enough to really grip it—use your knife at the beginning if you have to. Once you get started, the hide will come off simply by using the mechanical force of your hands. Use your fists to get under the hide and really push to separate it. Avoid taking excessive meat off with the skin by using your brute force to guide it as it goes. Pulling, fisting and prying will do the job. This way there is no chance the hide will get cut by a blade, which is very important if the hide is going to be used for anything.

Smaller Creatures

The main difference in gutting and skinning smaller mammals is that for creatures rabbit-sized and smaller, the anus is so small that cutting it free as described above is impractical. Fortunately, the pelvic bone is weak enough that you can easily break through it by prying with your knife. After making a slit from the pelvis upward to the ribs or neck, remove the entrails from the cavity, leaving them attached to the colon. Shove your knife under the pelvic bone, beside the intestine that travels through this canal between the pelvis and sacrum, and pry upwards, breaking the bone so the colon can be easily accessed and removed. Otherwise, smaller mammals are for the most part processed the same as larger ones.

Birds

The bodies of birds differ considerably in their structure from those of mammals. The most significant difference for our purpose here is that they are feathered. You can skin birds as you skin mammals, but much of the fat on a bird's body is stored directly beneath the skin and will be removed if you do this. This would, in most instances, be foolish, as not only does this fat hold precious nutrition, it is the most delicious part of the bird. When you are processing birds, you will want to pluck them, which can be made easier by briefly submerging them in a hot water bath to loosen the feathers.

Heat a pot of water big enough to fit your bird in until it boils, but don't put the bird in yet. There should be enough water that the bird can be submerged, but not so much that it spills over the sides when you dunk the bird(s) under.

Once the water comes to a boil, remove it from heat. Into this very hot but not boiling water, submerge the bird until the feathers loosen—I usually count to 30, then remove the bird and pull. Various sources will say various lengths of time. Submerging a bird for too long will cause the skin to cook and come off with the feathers as you pluck. The hotter the water is, the shorter time you need to dunk, the cooler the water is, the longer. As you go along you will get a feel for it.

Gutting is simple and straightforward: simply make a slit from just above the anus to the breastbone, reach up into the cavity, grab hold of the lungs and pull the guts out. The intestines will still be attached at the anus; simply cut around the anus so it is detached from the body, and the guts will be fully removed.

CHAPTER 19

De-Industrializing Contraception: Birth Control for Sustainability and Survival

O VERPOPULATION is high on the list of problems endemic to civilization. In a healthy environment, the population of any species is kept in balance by natural forces. By using the tools of civilization and industrial society, however, humans have been able to remove many natural checks and balances, to the point where we are eradicating extraordinary amounts of non-human life, leaving wasteland and human monoculture in our wake.

The most affluent nations have been able to halt and even reverse population growth in some instances, while those peoples that are most marginalized have the greatest incidence of unplanned pregnancy and steep population growth.

The only methods of contraception most people know and trust require an industrial infrastructure. This is one reason there is a direct correlation between the wealth of nations and birth rates: industrial products are not as available in undeveloped nations. Not only do people need to be educated on safe sex and contraception, they also need access to contraceptives created a world away. This has serious implications in the event that such industrial infrastructure ceases to function. When we talk about a collapse, or even a soft transition into a sustainable way of life, we are talking about life without industrial production, which includes access to manufactured contraceptives. Condoms, the pill, the shot, spermicides, you name it. People will continue having sex, and even though living conditions will be far worse for having children, pregnancies and births will likely bloom. All because industrial society has created a monopoly on contraception, eradicating traditional methods.

Overpopulation is, of course, a problem of civilization. It was not an issue for sustainable indigenous cultures. Almost all indigenous cultures had effective, natural birth control practices that allowed them to decide when, or if, they would have children. This knowledge appears to be one of the first things colonizers seek to eradicate when assimilating traditional peoples. People that have unplanned pregnancies under difficult circumstances are more vulnerable. People that have control over when they reproduce are in a position of power.

Regardless of coming changes, knowing your body's rhythms, learning how to be intentional and in control of your fertility is incredibly empowering and important. For women, this means learning how to track your menstrual cycle — tuning into the bodily changes that occur before, during and after ovulation. It also means getting to know some abortifacient ("blood-moving") herbs, plants that promote menstruation (emmenagogues), as well as implantation inhibitors (morning-after-type herbs like wild carrot seed, discussed earlier in this book). To provide comprehensive information on all of this (fertility awareness, herbal abortion, etc.) is well beyond the scope of this book and, as someone who doesn't have a vagina, out of my field of experience.

For more information, see sisterzeus.com, a comprehensive online resource, or check your library for resources. Any book on how to boost fertility should show you how to monitor your fertility for the opposite purpose. The timely and safe use of implantation inhibitors and abortifacients is essential knowledge, widely available from credible, detailed online sources. Do your homework and talk to anyone you can that has some knowledge here; it is so important.

And for men that have heterosexual relationships? Male-bodied people generally take a passive role in contraception and birth control, not being the ones that get pregnant themselves. Without condoms or pharmaceuticals, is there anything a male can really do to prevent or reduce the likelihood of his sperm getting to that egg?

Yup.

Pulling Out

Pulling out (also known as coitus interruptus) is one of the most ancient, effective and nowadays totally discredited forms of natural contraception. Mention it in any serious discussion about natural methods of birth control and expect to be severely ridiculed. "It doesn't work!" they will say. Many people call it the "pull and pray" method, since one is apparently relying more on faith than any actual form of contraception. I think it is absolutely vital to clear up pulling out's bad rap so that men can finally take charge of their fertility.

Pulling Out Works?

Yes, the science is in folks—it does. According to recent studies ("Better than nothing or savvy risk reduction? The importance of withdrawal," Rachel Jones et. al., *Contraception*, 2009), when pulling out *is done properly* (we'll talk about that next), it has a failure rate of four percent. The condom, if used properly (no breaks, no spills), has a failure rate of two percent, not actually much better. They also found that "realistic estimates of typical use indicate that about 18% of couples will become pregnant in a year using withdrawal. These rates are only slightly less effective than male condoms, which have…typical-use failure rates of…17%." I don't know how much truth statistics can actually reveal on this subject, given how many factors are involved and depending on how the information is gathered. The reason I include them is because they show that pulling out is scientifically recognized to be quite comparable in its effectiveness to other more politically correct forms of contraception. In my own personal experience, and over years of talking to countless men and women that have used the pull out method carefully and appropriately, I have witnessed a failure rate much lower than that presented by these statistics.

Condoms are known to tear and leak. Having millions of sperm inside the vagina contained by only a thin layer of latex is risky business. When done properly every time, I see no reason why pulling out wouldn't be just as or more effective than condoms. Both have inherent weaknesses.

Pulling out offers little protection from sexually transmitted diseases (STDs), making it more of a method to practice with someone you are in a relationship with, though if you happen to be having unprotected sex with someone you don't really know, by all means pull out!

How It Works, and How It Doesn't

There are two main reasons that pulling out can fail: the pre-cum, or "Cowper's fluid," that the penis releases during sex, and lack of self-control. It is commonly thought that pre-cum contains viable semen; this is a half truth. The function of pre-cum is to de-acidify the urethra, since urine (acid) has been passing through it. The acidity of the urethra is a problem for semen, they need a specific pH and will die in an acidic environment. Pre-cum de-acidifies the pH of the urethra and makes it a more hospitable environment for the big load of semen that will be passing through soon. Pre-cum is also called Cowper's fluid because it is stored in the Cowper's gland; it doesn't actually come directly from the testicles. By the time the semen in pre-cum make it into the urethra, they are usually no longer viable because of the time lag. Any that might still be viable are destroyed by their journey in the still acidic urethra—a recipe for dead pre-cum!

The problem arises when, after pulling out and ejaculating, one begins to have sex again.

The man's urethra has been de-acidified now, making it much more likely that the pre-cum this time around will contain viable semen. How can one avoid this? Take a pee after you have ejaculated, re-acidifying your urethra. That way if you have sex again the pre-cum will not be viable. *This is extremely important!*

Can You Do It?

The other reason pulling out fails is that the man doesn't pull out—or doesn't pull out in time. The level of ecstasy during sex can sometimes make it difficult to be aware and ready. A certain level of self-control and discipline are required that many men apparently lack, or are too lazy to cultivate. My recommendation is to practice while masturbating. Make the choice with your whole body that ejaculating inside a vagina is not what you want—that is how kids are made. If you don't want to be making kids right now, ejaculate elsewhere. Really, pulling out is easy—don't be a lazy jerk! Pull out well before you start ejaculating, and aim well away from the vulva. Your belly, her belly, the grass, wherever—aim away. One can definitely have fantastic sex while using the pull-out method, and by developing more self-control you will only become a better lover.

The real issue is less about whether or not pulling out works and more about whether you understand how it works and can actually do it.

Pulling It All Together

When I first began using coitus interruptus as a method of birth control, my partner and I were not acting from a place of intelligence or understanding. We were both young and foolish, bad at communicating, highly sexual but not very smart (sounds like a lot of people, doesn't it?). In fact, I was initially convinced that it was only a matter of time before my partner would get pregnant, though she seemed unconcerned and I was young and naïve. So we continued. A close friend I confided in assured me that I was a fool for not using a condom. Yet, somehow, it kept working. Even with her not monitoring her fertility and us therefore almost definitely having sex while she was ovulating (not recommended), and routinely engaging in repeated sex (extremely not recommended!). I couldn't understand. Eventually I began researching it and found out that it *does* work, if done properly, just like any other form of contraception. And there is a potential for failure, just like any other method of contraception. *When used in conjunction with a woman monitoring her fertility, its effectiveness is greatly improved.*

If someone is uncomfortable having unprotected sex, don't try to convince them that you don't need a condom because "pulling out works." Explain how it can work and add it to the list of possible methods of contraception in a gentle, respectful way with no expectation or pressure. It is important for people to understand that pulling out works, and how it works, for the obvious reason that people are always going to have consensual unprotected sex, whether or not that is an intelligent, responsible decision.

Most men don't pull out because they think it makes no difference. This is a sad mistake. Pulling out is no panacea, but a thorough understanding of how it works can help males take control of their fertility and be intentional with where they put their seed, hugely reducing the likelihood of unintentional pregnancy. I know, it can be messy. So keep a rag handy, it's not a big deal.

A few years ago I posted an article online about the myths and truths of pulling out. A couple of the comments I received from readers are worth sharing here.

"I'm very fortunate to have a partner who's very in touch with her body and can tell when she's ovulating. We used the pull-out method combined with the rhythm method for years without any problems. When we decided we wanted to have a child, it only took a month to conceive (and we're both in our mid-30s). So we're both, obviously, pretty fertile, especially for our ages. It does work, and it is another way to encourage you to be in tune with your bodies."

"The pull and pray method was working out great for us, then we decided maybe we were playing with fire and decided to use condoms. First time using one in years and it broke and we now have a son! LOL. So yes it definitely can be effective!"

Natural Condoms

What about the old lambskin condom? Condoms made from lamb intestine have been used for at least hundreds of years, possibly much longer. They have advantages over latex condoms in that they are not allergenic and provide more sensation and a more natural feel. Much like pulling out, however, they do not protect against STDs. They can be purchased online or from specialty stores, but if you are having a lot of sex, you'll be dropping some coin.

Another advantage to the lambskin is that it could be produced on a small, non-industrial scale. I have never personally made lambskin condoms, but in researching them and having some experience playing around with creatures' intestines as well as with condoms, I can offer some approximation of how one might go about making them. I have cleaned intestines and made them into little balloons, and I suspect manufacturing condoms would be similar.

First, you need some intestine from a lamb-sized animal. Deer and goat fit this description, with younger animals possibly providing thinner intestine for extra sensation. Empty the intestine of its contents and rinse it extremely well. It is of the utmost importance to sufficiently sterilize the intestine if it's going to be involved with genitals. A wood ash lye could be used, or soap and warm water. Do not cook the intestine to sterilize it, this will weaken it. Now tie off the tip with a solid knot or two, and blow the condom up like a balloon, testing for leaks. If there are any, forget it and try again.

This sterile, leak proof condom could now be oiled and dried. Oiling the 'condom' will keep it supple, allowing it to form to the penis, and will lubricate it. Stuff the condom with some fabric or what have you so it can dry without being folded in on itself. After slipping it onto a hard penis, one could tie it securely to the trunk of the organ if needed, to ensure it does not slip off during intercourse. Try it first without ejaculating inside, to see if it holds up to the task.

This is all completely hypothetical, but hey, if the system goes down, it could provide some helpful hints for the post-collapse lover.

CHAPTER 20

Working with Skin

S KIN FROM THE CREATURES whose flesh we consume as food has traditionally been central to the material culture of human societies. We don't have to look back very far to find a time when buckskin pants were the durable garb of the common laborer, naturally bark-tanned leather was used to make waterproof footwear, and people's mattresses were simply soft, warm furs. Nowadays, the skins of creatures are almost always discarded without a thought. Only a tiny number of the six million deer killed annually in the US have their skins used.

In the context of non-industrial, sustainable technology, skin is an incredible resource, furnishing breathable clothing, waterproof material, extremely high-strength cord, glue, containers, shelter coverings and boat-building material. Plant fibers must be processed and then tightly woven to create fabric; the fibers in skin, however, are already tightly woven and far more durable than any plant fiber. All one need do is preserve the skin in a useable state; the job of creating it has already been done. This is far less labor intensive than working with plant fibers. Industrial processing methods are what have made plant-based fibers more feasible.

There are many ways of processing skin from something slimy and perishable into something stable and useful, but four main methods stand out: rawhide, brain tanning, bark tanning and hair-on furs. The modern equivalent of rawhide might be plastic or cardboard. Brain-tanned leather's modern equivalent would be cotton cloth, as it is soft, breathable and totally *not* waterproof. Bark-tanned leather's modern equivalent would be plastic, either the soft plastics that rain jackets and tarps are made from, or the harder plastics used for water bottles. And fur is, well, fur.

Before you can preserve a hide in any useable state, you need to scrape off whatever flesh and fat are clinging to it.

Fleshing

For hides of any size (deer, sheep, goat and larger) fleshing can be done most easily using a somewhat dull scraping tool and a fleshing beam: a chest-high pole, about one to one and a half feet in diameter, leaned against a tree or other upright surface.

The scraping tool can be any piece of metal or bone with a square edge. If its edge is sharp, it should be dulled. I have used the flat back edge of big serrated breadknifes, wrapping the end of the knife with tape to serve as a soft handle.

The fleshing beam leaned into the crotch of a tree with a deerskin draped over its top and pinned in place for scraping by the beam and tree.

The hide is pinned between the beam and tree, flesh side up. This way the hide is held in place while being draped over the beam, which provides a hard surface to scrape against. Hold your scraping tool at a 45 degree angle

Scraping tool.

to the skin, so that it digs in and under any flesh or fat, and draw it downwards, scraping towards yourself.

The rounded surface of the beam provides a small point of contact between the scraping tool and the skin, which allows you to apply concentrated pressure to one area at a time. The smaller the diameter of your fleshing beam, the smaller the point of contact between tool and skin, meaning you will be scraping a smaller area with each stroke, but with more force. Shift the hide around on the beam, occasionally changing where you have it pinned between beam and tree until all the flesh and fat have been removed.

A small fur tacked onto a board for drying.

Smaller skins can be tacked tightly to a board and scraped clean with a blade, held at a right angle to the skin so as to not slice through it. A rounded ulu-type knife, adze or scraper all work well; a knife will get the job done, too.

Rawhide

Rawhide is simply dried skin, with the flesh and usually the hair removed. It has been used traditionally to make drums, for skin-on-frame kayaks, containers, super-strong cord, armor, roofing and even windows. Making it is quite simple, and most of the steps are also required for any other method of using a skin. If you would like to leave the hair on, simply allow your fleshed skin to dry, stretched, so it cannot shrink and fold up on itself as it dries, but dries out completely flat instead. You can accomplish this by tacking it, flesh side facing out, onto a plank, plywood or board with nails or pegs, or by poking holes with a knife along the edge of the hide, every four to six inches, and lacing it into

Poking holes with a knife, parallel to the edge of the skin, one inch in from the edge.

a frame. This is a basic method to preserve hides for storage as well, with the fat, flesh and moisture removed.

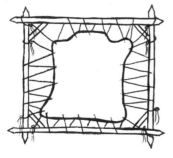

Skin laced into a frame.

Note that there are four separate cords lacing the four individual sides, tied off to the frame. To lace the hide into the frame, work on the ground and start by lacing the top (neck) end of the hide to one of the frame's four ends and tying it off. Then lace the bottom (butt) end of the hide to the opposite side of the frame and tie it off. Now lace the two sides of the skin in tight and retighten the top and bottom if need be.

To remove the hair, the hide can be left in a puddle or bucket until the hair slips or pulls out very easily, or soaked in a bucking solution, a mixture of wood ash and water. Soaking it in a puddle has the advantage of being effortless, while bucking has the advantage of being antibacterial—the hide will not rot—and so it is more controlled and predictable. A bucking solution is highly alkaline and cleanses the mucus membranes of the skin and loosens the hair. People have traditionally used wood ash lye as a powerful cleaner—pioneers would soak their clothing or linens in a "buck" once a year as a kind of old-time bleach.

To prepare a wood ash buck using hardwood ashes, start by mixing, in a bucket or other non-metallic container, two parts wood ash to one part water (start with two gallons ash to one gallon water). Mix well and let settle for 15 minutes. Hardwood ashes are quite alkaline, and if you make the solution too strong, it will eat away at the skin. If it's not strong enough, it will take longer for the hair to slip, or come out easily, and the hide may begin to rot during soaking. After letting it settle, test its strength by placing an egg in the buck. If it is the appropriate strength, the egg will float to the surface and poke its top above the surface, revealing an area the diameter of a quarter. If it is too weak, the egg will not float to the surface; if it is too strong, it will rise to the surface and either poke through, revealing a surface greater in diameter than a quarter, or will turn on its side. Add more ash if it's too weak, dilute with water if too strong, mix well and allow to settle another 15 minutes before testing again. All of this fiddling will produce an alkaline solution that is the perfect pH for our uses.

The floating egg test.

Submerge a fleshed skin in this bucking solution until the hair comes out with very little effort when tugged—two to seven days depending on temperature. Don't leave it for too long, as the alkali will eventually eat away at the skin and degrade it. When you remove the hide from the buck, wring it out, saving as much of the liquid as possible—it is very much reusable.

Now, with the hair loosened from the skin, take it back to your fleshing beam and this time drape it over with the hair side up. Using your dull scraping tool, or your hands, gently remove the hair and epidermis (a very thin layer of greyish scum that usually comes off imperceptibly with the hair).

With the hair removed, if you bucked the hide you must now rinse the alkalinity out by placing it in moving water overnight.

Dry your rawhide by stretching it out in a frame or tacking it to a board as described above. Rawhide can be rolled up and stored in a dry place indefinitely.

Bark-Tan Leather

By treating raw animal skin with tannin, an astringent phytochemical (plant constituent) found in many tree barks, one can create leather that is durable, rot resistant and water repellent to completely waterproof. The astringent tannins bind to

Bark-tanned deer leather, 100 percent local, wild and non-toxic.

proteins in the skin, altering the skin chemically, dyeing it a darker color and making it stronger and stable. Bark-tanned leather has traditionally been used in the manufacture of footwear, rain slickers, leather jackets, belts, harnesses, containers and more. It can be very soft and supple, or very thick and rigid, depending on how it is treated and the skin used. To fully explore this subject would require a book unto itself. Since that book doesn't currently exist, I will briefly describe the most basic method of turning a deerskin into luxurious bark-tan leather, giving enough detail that you will be able to reliably make leather and begin experimenting on your own.

Tanning

Do all of the steps for rawhide, above (except drying), preferably removing the hair by bucking; the alkaline soak cleanses glues out of the hide allowing tannin to enter its fibers more easily and resulting in softer leather.

Make a strong, tannin-rich tea using a tannin-rich bark: hemlock (my favorite), spruce, oak, fir, aspen, birch and alder are all good options, with at least one of each growing in most temperate areas. Tree barks contain the most tannin in spring, making that season the best for harvesting it, but they are useable any time of year. Chop the bark into small, bite-sized or finer pieces with a hatchet. The smaller the better, as far as extracting tannin. Fill a large stockpot half full with this chopped bark, and then to the top with "soft" water—rain or river water. Groundwater ("hard" water) has a mineral content that will create marks on the tanned leather, purely a superficial concern, but easily avoided by using surface water. Gently simmer for one hour, pour the tea into a large container and rebrew. Pour this second brew off and repeat once more if you like, for somewhat longer. The tea should be dark and quite astringent when you taste it. If it makes your mouth feel like it is being tanned, that is a sign of its strength. You will use this bark tea as a tannin-rich bath to submerge your de-haired skin in.

A thin deer skin can be placed in a vessel with full-strength tea, but usually it is diluted 50 percent with water. Thick skins, like cow, will not tan properly if they are put into a full-strength tea. They will simply tan at the surface, but the interior of the skin will remain untanned. To avoid this, thick skins are put into a very dilute tea, a vessel of mostly water with a bit of tea added. This is periodically strengthened by adding more full-strength tea slowly over six to twelve months. Deer skins, being thinner, can go into strong tea right away, and be done tanning in one to two weeks.

Submerge the skin in tea in a plastic or wooden tub wide enough that your deerskin won't be folded and scrunched up. If your deerskin is quite thin, you can put it into full-strength tea right away; if it's a bit thick, dilute the tea 1:1 with water. Add a quart of strong tea to your tanning bath every few days if you diluted with water.

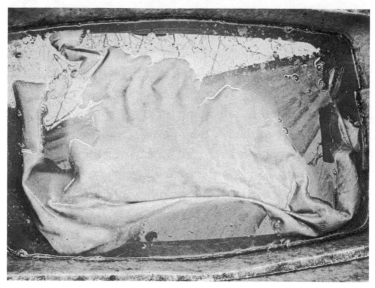

Deer skin in a hemlock bark tea bath.

Your skin should take on some color quite quickly; in full-strength tea, the whole exterior will be fully dyed within a couple of hours to a couple of days.

After a few days, pull the skin out of the bath and take it back to your fleshing beam. Lay it over the beam, this time with the flesh side facing up, and using a dull scraper remove any remaining membrane. There may be a lot, or there may be very little. Removing this will ensure the skin gets tanned through more easily. Lay a towel or something similar on the beam before this step to act as a cushion between the skin and the hard beam. This will prevent the grain of the finished leather from being marked. After scraping, place the skin back in the tannin bath to continue soaking.

Every few days, snip a little piece off one of the thickest edges of the skin, around the neck or legs. Observe the cross-section of the skin's fibers; look to see if any color from the tannin bath has made its way through to the interior of the skin. If it is still whitish-blue in the middle, it needs to tan longer. If it is at all tan-colored in the center, it is done tanning; tannin has penetrated into all of the fibers. It doesn't need to be completely dark in the middle, any amount of color at the

Cross-section of cow skin during tanning. Tannin has struck to the core of the upper piece of skin, indicating it is done tanning. The lower piece is still completely white at its core, meaning it needs more time. Thicker skin like cow must be tanned slowly and with greater care in diluted, weak bark-tea baths.

skin's core means tannin has penetrated all of the skin's fibers and it is functionally done.

Another old test is to take a snip from a thick area, as above, and apply saliva to it. If the skin soaks up the saliva it is said to be done.

If you are using a strong tannin bath, remove the skin immediately once it has tanned through, or it will over-tan and when you soften it the pretty grain will be brittle and crack.

Once your skin has tanned through, remove it from the tannin bath (which can be saved and reused) and let it rinse in moving water for a few hours—weigh it down with rocks to be cleansed in a creek or river.

Softening

Softening, the final step in creating leather, will determine how flexible and soft the finished product will be. It is achieved by applying oil to the tanned skin while it is damp and stretching and realigning its fibers while it dries. This way the skin will not dry hard and stiff like rawhide; instead, the oil will work its way between the fibers and lubricate them.

After rinsing your tanned skin, take it back to the fleshing beam. Drape it over the beam with the flesh side up, using a towel or other cushioning between the beam and skin. Again, this is to prevent the grain of the skin from being permanently marked by the beam. Using your dull scraping tool, gently squeegee as much water out of the skin as possible. Now, take it someplace warm like a sunny spot or near the wood stove. You want the hide to start drying out slightly before you apply oil, just enough so that it will readily absorb it.

Oils I have used for softening leather include lard, olive oil, fish and sea mammal oils (they will smell), bear fat, coconut oil and tallow, which sometimes leaves more of an oily film on the leather. Semi-solid and liquid oils work best. Only pure oils are used with bark-tanned leather, not brains, which contain emulsified oil.

Melt your oil (unless it is already liquid at room temperature) and apply it (once it has cooled) by laying the damp skin down flat and rubbing in the oil. Apply it liberally, but only as much as the skin can absorb. Now alternate between stretching the skin, realigning its fibers, working it over the back of a chair or staking post, letting it sit and dry and applying more oil if it looks like it can soak it up. You want to keep the fibers moving, realigning and stretching apart, but also let the skin continue to dry by being in a warm, airy, open (not scrunched up) situation. Keep it too cool and you will be working forever; let it dry too quickly and you won't be able to keep pace. Find that happy medium.

Softening a skin by hand-stretching with a friend.

Methodically stretch all areas of the skin over the back of a chair, staking post or similar dull-edged surface, focusing more energy on the areas that are drying out fastest (the thinner spots). Get a friend to grab one side of the skin and pull to stretch it out, or do this as best you can on your own, over your knees or just between your hands, separating those fibers from one another.

If all works out, your stretching and oiling will result in supple leather once the skin has dried. If there are stiff spots, simply re-wet them and work them again while they dry, whenever you feel like it.

There are many instances where a stiffer leather is desired. For this, simply don't put as much energy into the softening.

The staking post, an excellent tool for stretching and softening skins.

The application of oil is actually what makes bark-tanned leather water repellent or waterproof; if you want your leather to be more water-repellent, simply apply more oil. Tallow was traditionally used for more waterproof leathers, but most all heavily oiled leather will shed water well.

Staking post in action.

Buckskin

Buckskin or brain-tanned leather is soft, breathable, strong and comfortable for clothing. Because its manufacture has been covered so well by other authors, I will not discuss it here, except to say it is a craft well worth learning and a wonderful material. There are many excellent resources available to the would-be brain tanner, the best of which, by far, is the fantastic *Deerskins into Buckskins* by Matt Richards.

Brain Tanning Furs

To go into all the different techniques required for various furs is too broad a subject for this book. There are some skins that are most useful and easily tanned with the

Bark-tanned deerskin mittens, with an inner liner of rabbit fur. Biodegradable, sustainable and beautiful.

hair on, however, and tanning skins with their hair on is usually quite straightforward. Here is the process for a rabbit skin, which can be applied to many similar creatures.

Tack the skin to a board and flesh as per above. Allow the skin to dry tacked up tight like this. After it has dried, take a sharp tool (knife, adze, scraper) and, holding the blade at a right angle to the skin, scrape away the thin layer of membrane coating it. This will allow the skin to soak up a solution of brains or what have you more easily and turn out softer. Be *very* careful not to scrape right through the skin, just remove this thin layer of membrane. Sometimes it will peel off in strips once you get it started. Don't get carried away.

"Braining" and Softening

Now apply a solution of either brains, eggs or soap and oil. All of these fats work equally well. Soap is added to oil to emulsify it and draw it into the skin, where the oil in eggs and brains is already emulsified. Prepare this solution by mixing, if you are tanning a rabbit skin, one rabbit brain (or one or two egg yolks) with a quarter cup of warm water. Mix and mash this into a well-blended soup. Now apply this to your dried skin, getting it to soak up as much as it can, until it is fully rehydrated.

The job ahead now is softening, which is done much the same way as for bark tanning. While the skin goes from wet to dry, keep those fibers moving, stretching and re-aligning, using a staking post, the back of a chair, your knees or just your hands. For tanning furs, abrading the flesh side of the skin can help produce a softer end product. Use a pumice on it periodically, as if you were scrubbing some dead skin off in the bath, or

Using the softening cable to stretch a small fur. Only the flesh side is pulled against the abrasive cable.

a softening cable. Small furs don't take much time or effort, provided they can dry out.

To make a softening cable, use aircraft cable and steel nuts. Bend the cable to form loops at both ends, slide a metal nut over this loop and hammer it flat, securing the loop in place. Aircraft cable can be found at hardware stores; natural alternatives would be rawhide cord or a bowed hardwood pole with an edge carved into it or piece of slate embedded in it.

How to make a softening cable.

Smoking

Now that you have a softened fur, in order to preserve that softness and ensure that if the fur gets wet it will dry supple, you have to smoke it. Smoke chemically changes the skin's fiber structure, making your softening permanent. Smoking has nothing to do with waterproofing. Smoked buckskin, for instance, is about as waterproof as cotton (it's not waterproof at all). For smoking larger skins, refer to Matt Richards' *Deerskins into Buckskins.* To smoke small skins, you could hang them in a smokehouse for a day or more, if you or someone you know is smoking food, or you can make an intentionally smoky fire. The instructions below may seem elaborate, but they can transform smoking a skin from an arduous, stressful, multiday affair, to a half-hour to hour of fun.

Not being a purist, I prefer to use a smudge pot for smoking skins—a big old pot that I can start a fire in. Get a good fire going in your smudge pot, working up to nearly wrist-thick pieces of wood, preferably a hardwood so you get a good bed of coals. Let this blaze burn nearly down to coals, then smother the glowing, lively embers with golf-ball to fist-sized chunks of dry, punky (rotten) wood (see the chapter "Fire and Light" for more on punky wood). This produces copious amounts of smoke, perfect for getting the job done. Make sure you really do smother your fire with the punky wood, you want it to smoke profusely, but still be covered enough in punk that it won't readily burst back to flame.

By using a smudge pot, one reduces the risk that the fire will flare up, since the container seals it off at the bottom and sides from oxygen. If you don't have a pot, digging a hole into the ground would be the alternative. You want to funnel the smoke, instead of letting it disperse and go to waste, so it can be soaking into your skin. The smudge pot also facilitates this beautifully. My preferred setup employs a piece of plywood, with a hole cut in its center, placed like a lid over the smoking smudge. An old chunk of stovepipe can be placed over the hole in this plywood, creating an effective funnel to concentrate the smoke.

A luxury smoking setup.

If you have multiple furs, they can be roughly stitched (or glued using hide glue or non-toxic, white goopy school glue) into a sack together and suspended over this setup, flesh side facing in. For the purpose of extra insurance and to ease the smoke into the right place, attach a skirt to the base of your sack of furs by stitching or gluing. This skirt can simply be a pant leg, or whatever fabric you have that can go over the smoky stovepipe and funnel smoke into the skins.

In the illustrated setup, the skin sack is suspended above the smudge pot, a skirt is attached to the skin sack and tied off to a piece of stovepipe. A board with a hole cut in its center directs the smoke into this apparatus. If you don't have a big, thick pot to dedicate to this, simply dig a hole in the ground for your smudge.

You only need to get smoke into the flesh side of your fur, and once it takes some color, really any amount of color, it is functionally done. The more you smoke it, the darker it will get, and the more it will reek of smoke. It may take ten minutes or a few hours depending on your setup and other variables. Check the inside of your sack after ten or twenty minutes to see if there is any color.

Stay right there with your skins as they smoke. If the smudge bursts into flame suddenly, you'll want to yank your precious furs to safety. Add punky wood as needed. If you started with a good bed of coals, the wood should simply turn into coal, allowing you to add more and continue the smudge for quite a while. Gluing your hides together into sacks will drastically reduce the amount of time smoking takes, as the smoke will be better sealed into the sack.

Let smoked skins hang outside to air out for a day or so to mellow their scent.

Jello

If all this tanning sounds like too much work, but you still want to make use of a skin, why not make jello out of it? Jello can be made from skin and is a highly nutritious and delicious dessert.

To make it, ideally you would prepare the skin as per rawhide above, allowing it to dry completely. Drying out seems to change the proteins in the skin, making the glues in it more extractable. After drying, cut thin strips or chunks off the hide for making the jello. Place the dried strips in a pot and cover with water. Allow them to rehydrate overnight. After they have rehydrated, bring to a very gentle simmer, and allow to brew for at least four hours, preferably longer. Add water if necessary. Add any flavors while it is brewing—berries, juice, sweetener, etc. Let it cool several hours or overnight, until it sets. You will be very popular with your friends.

Jello is prized in traditional Chinese medicine as one of the best yin tonics, that is to say it nourishes the material essence of the body, providing building blocks for skin, cartilage, tendons and bodily fluids.

It is also the basis for natural, water-soluble hide glue. Make an extra-strong jello and allow it to cool and set. This can then be sliced into chunks and dried on screens some place warm. If you need glue, simply rehydrate in just enough warm water (don't cook it) to get it to a syrup consistency you can apply with a brush. It works amazingly well, but keep in mind it is quite water soluble, which is good if you glue your fingers together.

CHAPTER 21

Getting to Know Nuts

A CORNS AND TREE NUTS had a significant place in traditional human diets wherever they abound. Perennial,
long-lived, calorie-dense plant foods that are easily gathered
and preserved, nuts and acorns are an incredible source of
nutrition.

Harvesting and Curing Nuts (Including Acorns)

There are many, many species of edible tree nuts—here I will
mention just a few that are widespread. Processing and preserving techniques are generally similar for most nuts. After
harvesting, in order to store nuts for any length of time, they
need to be dried or cured. Below are notes on processing and
preserving several species.

Hazelnuts

If you live somewhere with large populations of squirrel or
other nut-crazy creatures, you can ensure your own harvest by
gathering still-green hazelnuts off the tree before they have
fallen, while they are still in the husk. Let them ripen some
place warm and dry and, of course, protected from squirrels.
Otherwise, let them fall on the ground and gather. If the
ground is somewhat barren, you can sometimes rake them into

piles, which is incredibly satisfying. You also won't have the added job of de-husking nuts if they fall naturally.

Fresh hazelnuts taste like coconut or water chestnut, really good, but for preservation they need to be dried or else will rot. To dry them, you can spread out a layer of nuts on whatever unused, sheltered, creature-proof surface you have and let them sit for a month more or less, depending on temperature, or put them on screens above the wood stove or someplace warm to dry faster. The easiest way is to put them in mesh sacks (free from any grocery store, just ask for some old onion sacks), about one quarter full, and hang them in a good warm place. Shift the nuts around every couple of days to ensure even drying. A sustainable alternative to mesh sacks could be large woven willow baskets.

Once dry, the nuts can be stored indefinitely in sacks. Hazelnuts will stay good for a surprisingly long time if kept in the shell. We've stored them for three years, and they still weren't rancid. That is really long! It makes them one of the most storable, nutritious foods, considering all you need to store them is to let them dry out. They will go rancid faster if they get too hot (like roasted) while being cured. They will also get much tastier, though.

They taste better, and are much more nutritious, if, after being shelled, they are soaked in water for eight hours or roasted before eating. These processes diminish phytic acid, an anti-nutrient which interferes with and blocks mineral metabolism. Soaking and roasting were practiced by indigenous cultures that used these nuts to any extent in their diet. Soaked nuts can be dried again for storage.

Walnuts

Treat walnuts in much the same way as hazelnuts. Since they grow on larger trees, gathering them while still green is not as feasible. Letting them fall and gathering them off the ground is more standard.

Walnuts have more of a tendency to mold than hazelnuts, so take care to dry them in a warm, well-ventilated situation. If you choose to dry them in mesh sacks or baskets, fill them only one-quarter full, make sure they are someplace warm (near a stove or furnace) and shift them around regularly. After they have cured, they will keep, in their shells, for a couple of years.

Walnuts contain more anti-nutrients than hazelnuts and are ideally soaked before eating. The soaking water will turn the color of very dark urine. They can be dried after soaking to restore crispiness.

Acorns

Acorns are the fruit of the oak tree, a staple food of indigenous cultures from northern California, the British Isles and many other far-flung places.

Acorns need the same considerations as listed above, and then some. They need to be dried quickly in the sun or by a heat source, or little grubs will infest them. This will reduce their shelf life considerably! They also contain large amounts of tannin that must be leached before they can be eaten. To accomplish this, remove their shells and lightly toast the nuts to get the outer skin to loosen and come off (this skin is very astringent). Then pulverize the nuts using a mortar and pestle, two rocks, a sturdy food processor, etc. into a fine meal. The finer the better, as the tannins will leach out more easily if the acorns are finely ground. This meal is put into a cloth sack. You could use a pillowcase, sock, etc.—traditionally, very finely woven baskets were used—tied closed and allowed to sit in running water for one day and up, depending on the variety of oak and how finely the meal was ground. Do a taste test every day. When there is no bitterness left, the acorns are ready. Acorn mush is prepared by adding water and cooking it as a kind of porridge. It's a lot of work, but tastes pretty good. Acorn meal can also be used to make flat cakes.

Though acorns require a considerable amount of work to process, since they are a wild tree nut that need only be harvested and processed, they are still more efficient, as far as energy invested vs. calories received, than most cultivated starchy staple foods.

Chestnuts

Before the great chestnut blight that hit America over a century ago, the chestnut was one of the most predominant trees of the Eastern woodlands. They are primarily a source of sweet starch, having a much lower oil and protein content than other nuts. This likely makes them more storable. The bristly husk chestnuts are encased in can discourage other creatures from harvesting them, but is easily opened by stepping on it. Though they no longer abound in the Eastern woodlands, Asian, European and American chestnut varieties have been planted in many areas of North America.

Fresh chestnuts are prepared by slicing an X into the shell and roasting. This can be done in an oven for about 15 minutes, or on top of a wood stove until the Xs you marked begin to swell and burst open. They are then peeled and eaten or prepared in other ways, for example, in traditional chestnut soups or stews.

Chestnuts can be stored fresh, without drying, for a couple of months in a cool dry place. They can also be dried in the same way as hazelnuts and other nuts described above, and either well rehydrated to be treated like fresh chestnuts, or peeled dry and roasted. They taste kind of like dried bananas eaten this way, and very sweet!

Horse Chestnuts

Horse chestnuts, also known as "buckeyes," have also been used traditionally as food by indigenous people in Japan, California, the Eastern woodlands and likely elsewhere.

They are toxic in their unadulterated natural state; traditionally they would be roasted, peeled, then ground into a meal and allowed to leach or sit in running water for several weeks. The moving water removes tannins, saponins and other inedible constituents, leaving behind mostly pure starch. They are ready to cook and eat when they are no longer bitter.

Score an X through the shell and roast as with chestnuts. They will swell and the Xs will burst open like chestnuts', though they will also bubble and ooze juices, likely toxins (saponins) if the smell they make while cooking is any indication. Peel and chop the nutmeat finely to dry; it may just conveniently crumble in your hands. This will take one to two days on a screen someplace warm. After drying, grind into a meal with a mortar and pestle, grain mill or what have you. Put into a pillowcase, sock, spruce-root basket or other finely woven receptacle and place in running water. Taste every few days in the course of a few weeks until the meal is no longer bitter at all (spitting it out if it is at all bitter), then use it however you please as a starchy meal (porridge, fry bread, etc.). As a porridge it is very creamy, like cream of wheat, and not great tasting, but not awful. This meal could be dried and stored for future use; it has a very low oil content and so should keep for a while.

Many North American cities are planted thickly with heavily producing horse chestnut trees; either it's part of the elite's plan to one day have us all eating horse chestnut mush in labor camps, or it is a fortunate, abundant source of food for hard times.

Plant Some!

Be smart like the squirrels and plant some of your harvest. If you want nuts to germinate well, don't dry or cure them at all, simply put them somewhere out in the wind, rain and cold after you harvest. Planting them shallowly in soil also works. Many varieties need to freeze before sprouting, so don't plant them too deep. Drying reduces seed viability considerably. In the spring they should start sprouting, and now you can move them to happy homes. Some trees will have a very high germination rate, others won't; paying attention to this can help you choose which trees' seeds have the best stock for planting.

Secondary Harvests

Where squirrels are abundant, often many tree nuts will mysteriously disappear the moment they ripen. Squirrels are so in touch with the nut trees' rhythms that the very moment they are ripe, the nuts can seemingly vanish. Where I live this problem doesn't currently exist, though further south on Vancouver Island the eastern grey squirrel has been introduced, effectively harvesting almost all of the nuts in its range. As the permaculture saying goes: "The problem is the solution." By harvesting squirrels for food one can turn a problem into another source of nourishment.

Squirrels are excellent food. They are a great source of wild protein, minerals and fats. Roasted squirrel is a delicacy; the bones are often small enough that they can simply be chewed well (crunch, crunch) with the meat, providing a direct source of calcium, magnesium and other bone-building nutrients. Some larger squirrels may need to be stewed for you to extract the minerals from their bones. Adding the head to the stew will make a richer broth, valuable oils from the brain coming out in it.

Nut trees are like bait stations for trapping squirrels.

CHAPTER 22

Exploring Entomophagy: Bugs as Food

INSECTS ARE A COMMON feature of cuisines across the world. Asian, North, South and Central American, African, Australian—nearly all cultures have incorporated insects into their diet to some degree. Eighty percent of the human population on Earth incorporates bugs into their diet in some way.

Even in Westernized countries, insects are consumed by everyone, daily—we just don't know it! Food regulations don't prohibit the "contamination" of grain or other foodstuffs by insects. It is well-known that all grain contains small amounts of dead insects or insect larvae; according to the US Food and Drug Administration, 100 grams of wheat flour contain an average of 150 insect parts. This contamination has traditionally been an important source of protein, vitamins and minerals for "vegetarian" cultures.

Insects are the epitome of a whole food, as they are typically eaten whole. One is eating all of the body's elements—flesh, fat, organs, blood and bones (exoskeleton)—thereby getting top quality protein, amino acids, vitamins and minerals. Insect larvae contain very dense nutrients, much like the eggs of any creature. They are typically sources of the much-prized omega 3-fatty acids. They also contain vitamins A and D, as well as vitamin K2, a combination of nutrients that Dr. Weston Price's research found halted and reversed tooth decay, among other degenerative conditions. As a survival food, insects, in season and where they abound, are absolutely vital.

Intentionally consuming insects as food, however, is not often practiced or accepted in Western society. It is the stuff of macho daredevil reality TV shows. Exploring entomophagy (eating insects), however, has the potential to open up wild, sustainable, healthy sources of dense nutrition all around us, many of which people generally see as nuisances and vegetarians and omnivores, the ecologically aware and unaware, thoughtlessly curse and smush.

"Entomophagy" specifically refers to consuming arthropods as food, which is broader than insects; it includes most creatures with exoskeletons, segmented bodies and jointed appendages. But scientific definitions aside, bugs are bugs. I have included some "little ones" here that do not by any means fit into the arthropod category. Here's some information on what bugs to eat. Apparently there are over 1,700 known edible species, so this is by no means a complete picture of the possibilities, but more of an invitation to explore.

Rules of the Game

There are a couple of things to keep in mind while exploring:

- Some insects are toxic; a general guideline is that brightly coloured species are more suspect, while those clad in darker, camouflaged earth tones are safer. Likewise those that are hairy are suspect and unpalatable (their little hairs can be really uncomfortable in the mouth).
- Insects are sometimes sprayed with insecticide; avoid harvesting from areas where this might occur (e.g., conventional farms).

- Urban insects are suspect; in moments of need they are a valuable food source, but for everyday eating try to stick with healthy bugs, not the cockroaches from the bottom of the dumpster.
- A bug net can be a great harvesting tool.

A Handful of Edible Species

Where I live there are definitely edible insects, but not in the same variation and abundance as other bioregions. I've read accounts of Paiute food gatherers burning a field of grass to expose (and roast) large quantities of grasshoppers, and indigenous Peruvians harvesting large amounts of edible tarantulas (with large, fatty butts) from caves. The insects I mention here are widely distributed, but perhaps where you live there is an abundance of a certain edible species specific to that area? It's worth looking into.

Ants

Ants are the first wild animal I ever killed and ate, at the age of four. Most ant species are edible, their flavor is pleasantly sour. This is because ants secrete an acid when threatened, giving them a vinegar-like flavor. In Colombia ants are roasted with salt (crunchy salt-and-vinegar ants!) and eaten at feasts. The queen ants are preferred there, having big juicy butts (more fat). In Colombian folk culture, queen ants are said to boost libido.

Ant larvae are also fantastic, having no sour flavor. They can often be found in clumps under rocks, or on top of anthills when they are being moved or kept warm.

To harvest ants, one can put a stick on an anthill, wait for it to get covered with ants, then shake it off into a container. A lid on the container will suffocate them, but this death may

allow them to secrete more acid. Roasting them right away
will kill them more quickly and prevent this.

Slugs

Slugs—food? Yes, slugs are edible and, if anything like their
cousin, the snail, highly nutritious (somehow nobody has done
a study on their nutrient content yet). They are not insects,
but come close enough (being small and crawly) to make an
appearance here. Every gardener knows how abundant a food
source slugs are for the warm, wet months of the year. While
there are no mysteries to reveal about harvesting slugs, there
are a few things you should know about preparing them.

Slugs (and snails) are host to a potentially dangerous parasite called the rat lungworm. They contract this parasite by
eating the feces of infected rodents. If a human eats raw snail
or slug, these parasites will not live in their body, but it can
produce a toxic reaction called eosinophilic meningitis. Meningitis is an inflammation of the meninges, a sheath surrounding the brain, and can cause severe brain damage. How do we
avoid this and still eat snails and slugs? Cook them! It's as
simple as that.

Slugs also sometimes eat things we can't—toxic plants and
fungi, poo, etc., so the traditional method of preparing them
for the table has been to purge their digestive system. For escargots this is done by putting snails in a container with cornmeal, oats or some other bland starch for a week, so they poop
out anything that might be offensive and fatten up on grain.
I've never had the heart to do this. For slugs I think it makes
most sense to simply gut them and skip the whole purging
process. To gut, kill the slug by chopping its head off, then
simply squeeze out the entrails. The slug will shrink considerably, and you will get slime on your hands.

How to cook them? Chopped up in a stew is a pretty good

option, or roasted over the fire or chopped, marinated and sautéed — experiment!

Snails

Snails of course have a rich and continuous tradition as food, the famed French escargots being a dish most of us are familiar with, whether or not we have consumed it. The common garden snail was introduced from Europe as a food source. All of the above cautions around eating slugs raw apply to snails, which, as mentioned above, have typically been purged and fattened on grain (cornmeal, oats) for a period of one to two weeks before consumption. Snails do not seem to be as merdiverous as slugs (they don't eat as much shit), though they may still consume vegetation or fungi toxic to humans. To ensure snails are safe to eat, steam them and remove from the shell, then slit up the belly and remove the cooked entrails. Or you could purge them for a couple of days in a container with some food they like — vegetation, aspen bark or the traditional grain feed. If you know the area you are harvesting them from is not host to any toxic plants and feel confident in this, you can opt to not worry about it.

Snails are abundant in spring and can often be found in good numbers where they have a good food source. The usual method of preparation is to steam them five to ten minutes, remove from the shell and sauté. They are quite tasty, though if you leave the guts in and they have been eating bark (one of their favorite foods), they will have some astringent flavor.

Crickets

Inhabitants of open meadows, grassland, fields and some forests, crickets also have a continuous tradition as human food. They are sold by the pound, dried, in Mexican markets and fried or roasted before eating. Crickets are excellent pan-fried or oven toasted, with a bit of oil and salt if you like. The legs can be removed before eating as they are sometimes irritating. They can also be dried and stored for future use.

A simple trap for crickets a friend raised in Mazatlan shared with me can be set with nothing other than a Mason jar and some bait. Dig a small hole in the ground of a cricket-inhabited area, put the jar into this hole and move the soil back into place around it or simply put the jar on its side on the ground. A piece of bait is then placed in the jar (a slice of apple, oats, bread, carrot, lettuce, a bit of stale beer, try what you have). In the morning there should be some crickets enjoying themselves in there. Put the lid on the jar, with holes poked in if you want to keep them alive, and without if you want them to die.

As a variation, put water in the jar along with the bait and the crickets will drown. Often people use a solution of molasses and water or stale beer for this; other sweeteners or foods mixed with water may also work.

Grasshoppers

Grasshoppers inhabit similar terrain to the cricket and are similarly prepared and esteemed. They can be harvested by hand in the early morning before they are fully awake, using the same type of traps as described above for crickets, or using more ambitious methods.

In modern-day Uganda, there is a booming trade in grasshoppers; locals set up extensive grasshopper traps using tall, standing sheets of galvanized tin roofing, their ends stuffed into old oil drums and powerful lights shining on them at night. With the tin roofing reflecting light into the darkness, grasshoppers are attracted en masse to them, land on the upright, glowing roofing and slide into the old oil drums where they are captured.

I have friends that took part in a large grasshopper harvest in which a group of people holding hands formed a human wall and walked across a field of tall grass, herding grasshoppers into a tarp on the other end of the field. A good method to try if you have enough people.

A Mexican study recently compared the insect management strategies of several farms. Some of them used modern insecticides, others allowed locals to harvest grasshoppers for local markets. The two methods were equally effective in controlling grasshoppers, but one approach required money and poisoned the land, water and food being grown, while the other avoided those costs, providing healthy wild food and income.

Earthworms

Earthworms are highly nutritious, and, believe it or not, an invasive species introduced to the Americas from Europe.

Worms often come out en masse during heavy rains when the soil becomes so saturated with water they need to get out or drown. I have seen holes dug for fence posts in clay soil filled with water after a heavy rain, and the bodies of countless drowned worms. Doing this intentionally would be a way of trapping them.

Their bodies are filled with dirt, which can make worms sandy and unpleasant to eat. This dirt can be removed by purging (soaking them in water for 3–24 hours) or taking a worm in one hand and squeezing the dirt out of it with your free hand's fingers. After purging, their flavor can be a little bitter—not bad, but bitter. Drying them mellows this flavor; incorporating them into various dishes helps as well. They can be added to stir-fries, stews, anywhere your imagination wanders. Frying worms until crispy offsets their squiggliness, drying reduces their sliminess, making them more palatable.

Maggots

Yes, not only are maggots edible, they are a traditional super-food. They are also probably the most revolting insect one could imagine.

Traditionally, many cultures have relished maggots, leaving fish or meat out to become saturated with them and then eating the maggots raw. There is logic to this: a diet of exclusively lean meat causes severe health problems, eventually leading to kidney failure and death. This condition has traditionally been called "rabbit starvation." White trappers living in the north would often be afflicted as they attempted to live entirely off lean meat like rabbit, easily trapped in the northern forests, without sufficient fat or carbohydrates to balance the protein. They would get a kind of protein poisoning, diarrhea and malnutrition would ensue, and despite eating as much lean meat as possible, they would "starve" to death.

What does this have to do with maggots? They are capable of transforming lean meat into fat. Maggots are extremely fatty and a rich source of essential amino acids, making them nutritionally far more valuable than lean meat.

They don't have internal digestive systems of their own, so they secrete gastric juices directly onto meat, causing it to degrade or spoil (or "predigest" if you have a taste for it). That is why there is so much hysteria around maggots on meat, not because they make it unsafe to consume, but because they alter its flavor, texture and palatable shelf life.

Maggots will taste different depending on their food source. I have harvested them from meat that was left hanging for a bit too long, thrown them in a pan and fried them up. If they were on a rotting carcass with the guts and all still intact, they would have a stronger flavor. In any case, they are an acquired taste probably well worth acquiring. Their ability to transform lean meat into essential fats is both magical and potentially life-saving under certain conditions.

Someone once told me their grandfather, during the Depression of the 1930s, would take maggots that grew on a hunk of meat he kept in the cellar and spread them on toast like butter.

Aphids

Aphids are edible. Depending on what foliage they are feeding on, they can range from slightly bitter to sweet. Upon finding an infested plant or patch of plants, simply collect the aphids and eat them fresh or incorporate them into a meal as a nutritious supplement.

Termites

These little ones are another big player in traditional human cuisines. I have harvested them individually or in small groups and then toasted them in a hot pan. They have a high oil content relative to the size of their body and are quite tasty, with a slightly nutty flavor. Those with wings (called alates) are larger and fattier. In many areas where these alates are prolific, they are harvested using a lamp with netting around it. They are attracted to the light and will collect on the netting. The wings are shed easily, which you may have noticed if one has ever landed on you, and can be removed by winnowing after they have been toasted. A candle next to a mirror at dusk at the right time of year can yield some fantastic snacking. In old wooden homes infested with termites, this may be an excellent coping strategy. Sitting around with a friend and talking on the porch at sunset while catching some food in the warm summer night can be quite delightful.

Sowbugs

Sow bugs, also known as pillbugs and rolly pollies, are those little grey, pill-shaped mini-shrimp that you find when you lift up a rotten piece of wood, rock or anything that has been sitting on soil for a while. They are another nutritious bug to know, and are tastiest toasted and eaten crispy, though in a pinch you can eat them fresh.

Earwigs

Earwigs are edible and tasty too. Prepare them the same as termites or sowbugs. A couple of tactics for gathering them come from gardeners who disdain these little fellas.

Fill low-sided cans with a half inch of vegetable oil (or other liquid, food-grade oil) and place them on the ground. Earwigs will find their way in and drown. Or, alternatively, a beer bottle with a bit of stale beer left in it will attract earwigs. Strain, toast and serve.

All these species are just the tip of the iceberg in this field. So many insects are edible (cockroaches, many beetles, moth larvae, wasps, bees, scorpions and spiders—with their venom glands or stingers removed)—that to cover them sufficiently would be a book unto itself. As we connect more deeply to the land, and as we come to depend on it more directly for our subsistence and survival, seeing these little ones as food may help us immensely.

CHAPTER 23

Fire and Light

MOST SURVIVAL guidebooks gloss over enormous aspects of daily life; anything mundane often seems to be overlooked. In my quest for information on these finer aspects of everyday life, I naturally turned to texts on ethnobotany and ethnology, yet the scholars that put these together, too, seem to have had little interest in many fundamental, though mundane, aspects of daily living. For instance, where people on the Northwest coast pooed. Were there family poo spots? Personal latrines? What did they wipe with? Did they wash their hands afterwards? With what? It sounds mundane, but is actually one of the most important aspects of daily life.

Lighting is also among the top subjects on this list of neglected arts. Anyone who has spent a winter in the north without electricity understands how significant lighting is to daily life, for nearly half of the year at least. During the late spring, summer and early autumn, you can simply rise and fall with the sun. For those long, dark winter nights (and days if you live in a temperate rainforest) however, some lighting is essential. I know nothing of solar panels or mini-hydroelectric setups, though they sound nice. Fat- or oil-burning lamps are the only sustainable, soot-free form of lighting I have experience with.

They are incredibly simple, as or more effective than a good bright candle or kerosene lamp, and all the necessary materials can usually be gathered locally or scavenged.

Fat Lamps

I call these fat lamps because the term "oil lamp" is usually a reference to kerosene-burning lanterns, which put out a smell that's too toxic for me, and are actually not measurably brighter than this simple stone-age version. What these lamps burn is oil or fat from animal or plant sources.

I have seen old pictures of Inuit ice homes lit by oil lamps—beautifully carved, long shallow soapstone containers with many, many wicks burning at the same time, using whale or seal oil as a fuel source, the warm light reflecting off the rounded, white interior walls of the igloo. These oil lamps were actually used as a heat source and method of cooking by the Inuit, oil being a far more abundant fuel than wood in their bioregion.

There are three components: the lamp container, the oil and the wick. Suitable containers are anything that can hold oil and isn't flammable: oyster or large clam shells, a shallow ceramic container, a used shallow tin can, etc. I prefer a shallow clear glass container, a small mason jar for instance.

The oil can be rendered animal fat. Animal fats that are liquid or soft at room temperature are easiest to use (fish, raccoon, pig, seal, bear) while those that are solid (deer, cow, elk, moose, sheep, goat), also known as tallow, are a bit trickier to work with. Both can be used. Plant oils (dumpstered veggie oil, olive, canola, etc.) also work well.

The wick is made of a dry plant material that can soak up the oil and be lit on fire. This fire is meant to burn the oil, not the wick which sticks out of the oil enough for a small flame to glow, and through capillary action sucks oil from the container and up into the flame to keep it alight. One of the best wick materials is cattail seed fluff, which can be harvested in the fall and through the winter. After filling your lamp container two thirds full with oil, place a clump of cattail down in it. It will become saturated with oil but still float. Pinch some up above the surface of the oil—this is your wick.

The second best to cattail fluff is cedar inner bark twisted into two-ply cord. Experiment with whatever plant fibers you have available. Make a quarter-inch-diameter piece of cord, put it into your lamp to impregnate it with oil, then at the edge of your (non-flammable) container pull enough of the cord over the rim, resting on the rim, out of the oil and light. The flame will only travel down your wick till it reaches the rim. Adjust the flame by moving the wick in or out until you get to the sweet spot where the flame burns bright and clean with no soot.

A fat lamp in action, with a wick of plant fiber adjusted to provide the right size flame with the least amount of smoke.

If you are using a hard animal fat, heat it until it is melted, pour it into your lamp and then get the wick impregnated with oil and in place before the fat cools and solidifies. These lamps need to be tended regularly, the wick adjusted and the oil replenished as they both slowly turn into light. Use something non-flammable to adjust the flaming wick. You can also put multiple wicks in one lamp to intensify the light given off and fashion wire wick holders to keep the wick held steady above the oil, rather than just resting on the rim.

Fire

Fire has shaped human life beyond comprehension, facilitating the spread of humans into different regions and the utilization of different food sources like grains, starchy roots and many other plant foods that must be cooked to be digestible.

I don't offer a full description of firemaking techniques here. Many other books show you how to make fire from friction, as well as basic firemaking skills (*Northern Bushcraft* by Mors Kochanski has some of the most complete coverage of firemaking). Here I will just offer a few suggestions and tricks that could greatly help the feral homesteader, survivalist or backwoods trekker with fire.

Dead Wood

Dead wood has saved my life.

Okay, that might be a slight overstatement, but one of my first winters living in a cabin with a wood stove, my roommate and I cut down and bucked up an alder for firewood. The alder was still alive and green, but not knowing anything about seasoning wood (allowing the sap and moisture in the wood to evaporate before burning it), and having nothing else to use anyways, we attempted to make it work. It didn't. The wood would not keep a fire, it might hiss and sizzle as the water boiled out of it when it almost got going, but the wood was simply too wet to build or maintain a fire in our wood stove. We were screwed, both cold and suffering from smoke inhalation as we persisted in our attempts. That is until an acquaintance casually mentioned that standing dead trees had saved him more than once and that a standing dead tree will often be completely dry even in a rainforest winter, making excellent firewood.

We cut down a standing dead hemlock and were in business; the wood was completely dry and burnt amazingly. Now we could get a good fire going and stagger it with our wet alder. Since then I have relied on dead wood countless times, more than I would have liked to.

"Dead trees" are often more "alive" than those still living; they provide homes for birds, bats, insects, mycelium and countless others. Cutting them can be detrimental to the forest's health and should be done thoughtfully.

If you do not have seasoned firewood on hand, dead wood is often the only really viable option. This could be in a wilderness situation, or simply any situation where you rely on fire and haven't cut and seasoned wood in advance.

There are several things to look for. Coniferous trees are more resinous, meaning that they both catch fire more easily and rot more slowly. They will last much longer after dying before they are rotten and waterlogged. What you want is wood that is dead but not rotten. Any tree you find that meets those characteristics (chop into it and feel how dry the wood is) is a good find. Dead lower branches are good fuel, too.

In the temperate rainforests of the Northwest, if you can find a standing dead conifer, even in the middle of the endlessly rainy winter, you will likely have dry fuel to work with (for, among other things, drying wet fuel).

Deciduous trees vary in how well they season while standing dead. Because of their lack of rot-resistant resins, they begin to decay much faster. Maple is generally good, alder rots quickly, and birch bark is watertight and so seals the moisture into the wood, preventing it from ever fully seasoning after dying. In any case, chop into the tree and feel for dryness.

Keeping a Flame

Traditionally, people have not started fires every day. With high-tech fire-lighting tools like matches and lighters, starting a fire has become a simple, quick procedure; before these technologies, however, once a fire was started, it would often be kept for quite a long time, in the form of glowing coals.

A coal can be kept active for quite some time if it is deprived of oxygen and nestled in a medium that will slowly transform into coal. This medium is typically dry, punky (rotten) wood.

Punky wood can be found in any reasonably mature forest; look for rotten stumps or fallen, decaying logs. What you want are chunks of rotten wood that can be easily broken in the hand, but will not completely crumble into dust when handled.

To keep a coal alive, you can take two fist-sized chunks of punky wood, carve a small depression into one of them for your coal to fit into, sandwich the other one onto this and tie them together. Traditionally people in coastal areas would use clam shells with punky wood in them to transport coals, an ideal non-combustible container. Most conk mushrooms (chaga, tinder polypore, false tinder polypore, etc.) also hold coals for incredibly long. They should be dried before use.

Fireballs

Fireballs are highly combustible balls made from pine, spruce or fir pitch and the shredded inner bark of cedar or another similarly resinous tree. Once lit, they will burn steadily in poor conditions for long periods, plenty of time for damp fire materials to catch a flame.

Collect pitch either by looking for a wounded tree that has oozed out a good amount, or create a wound yourself. Yes, this hurts the tree — as much as me or you getting a very small cut hurts, probably.

Inner cedar bark can be found wherever there is a downed cedar. Remove a strip of bark and separate the inner fiber from the tough outer bark. Fluff it up or shred it with your knife. This can be done as a method of removing it from the outer bark. Using the knife at a right angle to the bark, scrape it along the inside, removing the inner bark pre-fluffed or shredded.

Melt down your pitch, mix it half and half with shredded

bark and form it into balls. These are an excellent addition to the backpack of anyone heading into the woods, wanting to be prepared. They can also be used as a source of lighting, producing a solid, strong glow for 5–20 minutes, depending on their size and the materials. They are better used outdoors or in a well-ventilated environment.

CHAPTER 24

The Tao Of Poo:
Notes On "Giving Back"

O NE OF THE MOST shocking aspects of modern life, and
there are many, is that we can't even accomplish something as simple as taking a dump without messing up. Industrial society has turned one of our body's most precious gifts
to the land, the main way that we keep the nutrient cycle un-
broken, into a toxic waste product. Instead of returning the
organic matter we daily take into our bodies to the soil, it
is flushed out of sight—often into rivers and the ocean after being "treated." This system is parasitic. Industrial society
gobbles up topsoil in the form of food and shits it into toilets,
stripping the Earth of organic matter that is then toxified
and mixed with clean water, contaminating that precious liquid too. Soil, the Earth's precious blanket, disappears, turned
into poison muck. The fact that it is the accepted norm for
us speaks volumes about how far Western civilization has run
astray from something resembling sanity.

Of course there are alternatives to flush toilets. Many books
have been dedicated to the subject of composting human poop
(most notably Joseph Jenkins' *The Humanure Handbook*). If
you want to compost your poo for garden use, I recommend

reading one of these manuals; the subject is too complex to cover here.

I will, however, share some notes on pooing in both wilderness and feral living situations. For some reason the subject of pooing is left out of most books on Earth skills, and anthropologists generally seem to have not bothered mentioning how indigenous cultures dealt with their poo.

A sustainable relationship with the land means shitting on it. Whether you are on a hike, camping, in a survival situation or living wild and free in the land, here are a few tips on how to poo responsibly.

On the Move

If you are hiking, camping, lost in the woods or in any other situation where you won't be pooing in the same area more than a few times, here is some protocol.

- Do not poo near water in low areas that might flood during heavy rains. The best poo spots are high, dry (above the water table) and 50-plus meters from any creek, river, etc.
- Poo like a cat: bury it. If you are pooing in a spot just once, dig or scratch a hole, poo and cover well. Some say you should cover it well enough so that you'd be comfortable sleeping with your head resting on it. I try to bury it deep enough so that no one stepping there will have a chance of getting crap on their shoes, but it will still be easily incorporated into the soil (six inches).
- Some recommend not covering your poo at all in outdoor situations. The argument for this is that people usually don't cover their poo very well, and really just camouflage it by barely covering it with debris, creating a booby trap for the unfortunate soul that walks by next. By not covering it at all, it is in sight and more easily avoided by future pedestrians. This is a good point, and in certain situations it

might be more appropriate. However, covering poo keeps flies from landing on it (and then landing on your food, which is bad news), dogs from eating it (and then licking you), and generally makes more sense in most situations. I would only recommend not covering your poo if you don't intend to bury it well enough that someone could walk over it without receiving an unpleasant surprise. In my opinion, it is always preferable to bury properly.

If you are going to be in an area for a bit, establish a poo spot. This could be a shallow trench with a pile of the soil you removed to make the trench beside it. Squat over the trench, make a deposit and cover with some of the soil. If this poo is properly covered every time, the trench should not smell at all. Two planks can be suspended over the trench to facilitate easy squatting. When the trench is getting near full, make sure it gets thoroughly covered with a good thick layer of soil, enough that you could sleep there and feel good about it. Plant a fruit tree on top. If this trench is made too deep, especially in a low-lying area, it may contaminate groundwater. As always with pooing, go somewhere high and dry.

An alternative poo-spot design is the above-ground poo spot. This requires no digging. Find or construct a perch to poo from, so you are raised off the ground. The poo is well covered with organic material (leaves, straw, sawdust, etc.). Again, if it is properly covered, there should be no smell. These spots can be used for quite a while, as this poo pile shrinks considerably as it decomposes. See the illustration for a useful design.

The above-ground poo spot. Poo is covered with leaves or other organic debris.

Wiping

Starting in late spring and ending in late fall, there are usually adequate leaves for wiping in most areas. Some of the very best are thimbleberry, burdock, maple and other large, soft leaves. The worst (excluding plants like nettle) is probably sunflower—ever rubbed sandpaper down there?

In the winter almost any non-abrasive plant material will work. Many mosses, fluffed-up inner cedar bark, fir or pine cones or a bundle of spent grass will do. See what is available in your bioregion and experiment. The infamous shit-stick is a good standby: find a smooth stick one to two inches in diameter and use it to wipe. This was the standard method of wiping in many areas traditionally. Snow is probably the best winter wiping material, if you can handle it. It really cleans things—you'll be pleasantly surprised!

Squatting

Not only have we forgotten that our poo is a source of precious fertility if put in the right place, we've also managed to forget how our bodies were designed to poo: by squatting. A large portion of humans on the planet still squat to poo; flush toilets in India and across much of Asia are squat toilets built into the floor and squatted over, not the thrones Westerners are used to lounging on.

Squatting.

Western medical science has found a significant correlation between hemorrhoids and sitting versus squatting during defecation. Sitting is also linked to an incomplete evacuation of the colon. The guts and colon are slightly kinked or contorted when you sit to poo, whereas when squatting, which our bodies spent millions of years evolving to do, the guts and colon are in a proper position to fully defecate. Constipation, colorectal cancer and other problems may be related to this.

I have been squatting exclusively for many years now. Even when I use a flush toilet, I lift the seat up and squat on the rim. It feels much too wonderful to ever go back to sitting. For some it might take a while to build up the flexibility and strength required to squat comfortably. If so, use something to hold onto while you are getting used to it.

When we see our poo as fertility and treat it as an offering back to the land, suddenly bowel movements take on another layer of meaning and beauty.

Diapers and Pads

Along the West Coast of North America, shredded cedar bark was used as a kind of bedding and diaper material in babies' cribs, though I wouldn't be surprised if some infants had adverse skin reactions to the harsh resins and essential oils it contains. Cattail seed fluff or down and other locally abundant, absorbent, soft plant materials were also used. Cattail down bedding could easily be kept clean and fresh in a crib; where a baby peed it would clump together and be easily removed. Menstruating women have used all the above fibers for menstrual pads. Absorbent cloth, of course, makes ideal, re-useable menstrual pads, and will probably be around for most of our lifetimes.

Conclusion:
The Future Primitive

*In the world I see, you are stalking elk through the damp
canyon forests around the ruins of Rockefeller Center.
You'll wear leather clothes that will last you the rest of your life.
You'll climb the wrist-thick kudzu vines that wrap the
Sears Tower. And when you look down, you'll see tiny figures
pounding corn, laying strips of venison on the empty car pool
lane of some abandoned superhighway.*

« Tyler Durden, *Fight Club* »

EVERYONE KNOWS that in any relationship, if there is a conflict that doesn't get dealt with, if someone is upset but doesn't speak up, things don't get better—they simmer and stew and get worse. If we don't stop and deal with our problems as they arise, making changes and course corrections while we go along, things are going to get more and more difficult until just existing in a miserable lie is too much to handle. Somehow, industrial society thinks it is immune to this law, that as it marches unflinchingly in one direction, that it calls "progress," there is no space for checking to see how things are going, let alone for course corrections. The myth of progress tells a story in which everything that came before this moment is useless and obsolete, while everything that comes after will be better.

217

No need to discuss, no need to slow down and check to make sure we are on the right course—everything is getting better, this is the law of life! If a person had this attitude in their human relationships, we might call them a deluded asshole.

Many will agree that the idea of progress, which is the ideological underpinning of civilization, is delusional, but still wonder where does it leave us if we completely throw that notion out. I would suggest that it leaves us with no limitations based on the idea of past and future. Without the idea of progress, ways of existing sustainably that humans employed in the past are no longer inferior. Instead of saying, "We can't go back to the Stone Age," we can simply and soberly look at what makes sense. There is no judgment based on who, where or when, but an honest evaluation of true sustainability. This honest evaluation could mean choosing to get in tune with one's body instead of taking pharmaceutical contraceptives; shutting off the electricity and just going to bed when the sun goes down; breathing fresh air, eating good food and getting enough sunlight instead of taking antidepressants; or killing a deer, eating its flesh and tanning its skin instead of importing exotic food and plastic raincoats.

This is the future primitive—a world where the lines of past, present and future are blurred. Where people have no ideological brainwashing that governs their actions, but instead treat all life and the wildness at its center as sacred.

I can think of nothing more exciting.

Index

Hawking, Stephen, 73
hazelnuts, 187–188
herbivores, 64
hides, 100, 151
horse chestnuts, 191
human manure, 136, 211–212
humans, evolution of, 11–13
Humanure Handbook, The, 211
hunter-gatherers, 6, 15–16, 21–22,
   27, 64, 133, 141–153
hypocrisy, 31–32

I
indigenous peoples, 12, 29, 36,
   47, 52, 63–65, 147, 164. *See also*
   hunter-gatherers; Native
   American cultures; traditional
   cultures, *and by name.*
industrial creatures, humans as,
   12–13
industrial farming, 61, 64, 67
insects, 193–202
Internet, 29, 36
Inuit, 65, 92–93, 119, 204
Iroquoi, 24, 139

J
jello, 185–186
Jenkins, Joseph, 211
jerky, 112–113

K
kale. *See* Gundru.
Kochanski, Mors, 206

L
Lakota, 48–49
lambskin condoms, 169–170
lamps, 203–205
land use, 20–22, 25–26, 35–36

M
MacKinnon, Andy, 77
maggots, 93, 95, 112–113, 200–201
marinades, 98
marrow, 63, 99–100, 117–118
McPherson, John, 150
meat, handling of, 91–101
medicinal plants, 123–131
menstrual pads, 215
Mestokosho, Mathieu, 27
mice, as food, 150–151
momentum, 37–38
monocultures, 5, 24, 35, 135
mouse traps, 150–152

N
Native American cultures, 14, 35.
   See also Great Plains.
non-renewable resources, 30
Northern Bushcraft, 206
Nutritional Bypass, The, 62
nuts, 187–192
Nuu-chah-nulth, 14

O
oil lamps, 204–205
omnivores, 65–66, 98–99
oppression, in society, 22, 25
Oregon grape, 129–131
organs, as food, 99–100, 113
overpopulation, 22, 23, 163, 164
ovulation, and veganism, 65–66

P
Pacific Northwest cultures, 25, 52–
   53, 133, 134, 141, 215
parasites, 98, 130–131
pastoral societies, 22
pathogens, 97, 98, 125, 150–151
patterns in nature, 19–20

sustainability, 3–9, 23
swales, 138–139

T
tallows, 92, 118, 119, 120, 180, 181, 204
tanning, 176–179
tannins, 128–129, 175–176
technology, 27–32
termites, 201
traditional cultures, 17–18, 25–26
trapping, 141–153
tree fruits, 104–106
tree planting, 138–139, 192, 213
trees, 206–208. *See also* tree fruit;s tree planting; wood.

U
undressing (skinning), 159–60
unlearning, 17–18
unstructured time, 37–38
USDA, 98

V
Vancouver Island, 35–36, 63, 192
veganism, 59–62, 65–68

vegetables, 106–110, 111, 137, 138, 140
vitamins, 66, 99, 100, 104, 105, 107, 113, 193–194

W
walnuts, 188–189
water storage, for fruit, 110–111
whites, in North America, 54–57
wicks, 204–205
wild carrot, 126–127
wild land base, 6, 25–26
wildness, and sustainability, 3–9
wood, 138, 206–208
wood ash buck, 174–175
wood stoves, 101, 104, 105, 113, 180, 188, 190, 206
Wounded Knee, 48–49
Wovoka, 47–48

Y
yarrow, 125–126

About the Author

MILES OLSON has spent the better part of the past decade living off the grid and intimately on the land, as a squatter on the forested edge of a sprawling town on Vancouver island. Subsisting by foraging, hunting, scavenging, gardening and scrounging as part of a small community of feral homesteaders, he has amassed a toolkit of endangered earth skills that are fast disappearing from this earth, as well as a unique perspective on the relationship between the human creature and wild nature, and the great winding road to a sane, sustainable way life.

If you have enjoyed *Unlearn, Rewild*,
you might also enjoy other

BOOKS TO BUILD A NEW SOCIETY

Our books provide positive solutions for people who
want to make a difference. We specialize in:

Sustainable Living ◆ Green Building ◆ Peak Oil
Renewable Energy ◆ Environment & Economy
Natural Building & Appropriate Technology
Progressive Leadership ◆ Resistance and Community
Educational & Parenting Resources

For a full list of NSP's titles, please call 1-800-567-6772
or check out our web site at:

www.newsociety.com

Printed in the USA
CPSIA information can be obtained
at www.ICGtesting.com
JSHW082159140824
68134JS00014B/331